ISBN 978-0-259-51175-5
PIBN 10820856

1 MONTH OF
FREE
READING

at

www.ForgottenBooks.com

By purchasing this book you are eligible for one month membership to ForgottenBooks.com, giving you unlimited access to our entire collection of over 1,000,000 titles via our web site and mobile apps.

To claim your free month visit:

www.forgottenbooks.com/free820856

English
Français
Deutsche
Italiano
Español
Português

www.forgottenbooks.com

Mythology Photography **Fiction**
Fishing Christianity **Art** Cooking
Essays Buddhism Freemasonry
Medicine **Biology** Music **Ancient**
Egypt Evolution Carpentry Physics
Dance Geology **Mathematics** Fitness
Shakespeare **Folklore** Yoga Marketing
Confidence Immortality Biographies
Poetry **Psychology** Witchcraft
Electronics Chemistry History **Law**
Accounting **Philosophy** Anthropology
Alchemy Drama Quantum Mechanics
Atheism Sexual Health **Ancient History**
Entrepreneurship Languages Sport
Paleontology Needlework Islam
Metaphysics Investment Archaeology
Parenting Statistics Criminology
Motivational

FOOLS
FOR CHRIST

Essays on the True, the Good, and the Beautiful

Jaroslav Pelikan

Impressions of
Kierkegaard, Paul, Dostoevsky, Luther, Nietzsche, Bach

FORTRESS PRESS

PHILADELPHIA, PENNSYLVANIA

CONTENTS

INTRODUCTION

These essays present a historical examination of several problems in the relation between Christian faith and human values—the True, the Good, and the Beautiful. The relation is a complex one. Sometimes it seems that Christian thought cannot do anything with the problem of value, but cannot do anything without it either. It is too dangerous to handle and too important to ignore.

The problem of value is dangerous to Christian thought because it has been peculiarly susceptible to idolatrous perversion. In values man has confronted an ultimate, perhaps even an absolute. Absolute Truth, the Highest Good, Ultimate Beauty are phrases which indicate that in the area of value there is something transcending—or at least something many have thought of as transcending—the relativities of ordinary exist-ence. In a sense, a value is greater than any man and would seem to participate in the nature of the Eternal. Yet in his metaphysics and ethics and aesthetics, man can manipulate a value and thus gain some control over the nature of the Eternal. The symmetry of truth in the great philosophical systems, the dazzling goodness of the great saints, the haunting beauty of the arts—all these fascinate us and allure us with a charm that may easily be mistaken for the holiness of God. From this fact we can understand why Christian thinkers have sometimes become idolatrous in handling the problem of value.

At the same time, this fact shows that the problem of value is too important to ignore. The goal of Christian faith is to subject the total life to God, to "take every thought captive to obey Christ." All life is under God, depending upon and subject to Him. Indeed, the very things which the natural mind makes the objects of its idolatrous worship become, for the mind of faith, instruments in the service of God. The idolatrous man may worship the state as though it were divine. Against this idolatry, exemplified in Roman emperor-worship and modern totalitarianism, Christianity has always protested. But while vigorously criticizing the deification of the state, Christianity has also insisted from the beginning that the ruler is "God's servant"—not indeed to be identified with God, but nevertheless to be seen in terms of the sovereignty of God. So also value is not God and cannot be a fit object of worship. Still the God whom faith has come to know as the Father of our Lord Jesus Christ lays His claim upon everything in life, including the True, the Good, and the Beautiful. "You shall love the Lord your God with all your heart, and with all your soul, and with all your mind." This demand surely includes our consideration of metaphysical, ethical, and aesthetic values.

Because of the complexity of this problem, the six thinkers discussed here seem to have something to say to contemporary Protestant thought. In his own way each has pointed up one or another aspect of the relation between Christianity and the problem of value: either the impossibility of equating the Holy with one or another value, or the necessity of subjecting all values to the Holy. All of them were drawn to an equation of the Holy with human value, but all came to realize, with existential dread, that God cannot be domesticated in a value. To the first trio—Kierkegaard, Dostoevsky, and Nietzsche—this realization came in the clarity of mind and singleness of heart that are the peculiar gift of the insane. Their insanity helped them to insights of which the normal and balanced mind is rarely capable. The other three—Paul, Luther, and Bach—may not have been insane in the clinical sense of the word. But by sacrificing themselves to the service of God and subordinating their values to the lordship of Christ, they evidenced the madness of the Holy, an insanity that saw what sanity refused to admit, the madness of which Paul was accused and to which he freely confessed when he labeled himself and his followers ever since "fools for Christ" (I Cor. 4:10).

CHAPTER I

THE HOLY AND THE TRUE

KIERKEGAARD

One of the values with which the Holy has frequently been identified is the True. It has been the peculiar temptation of systematic theology to make such an identification, and the history of Christian theology is replete with examples of the tendency to make faith equivalent to the acceptance of a set of truths.

From its very beginnings, the Christian church has faced this tendency. The Gnostic heresy, which seems to have appeared within the church during the first century, was an elaborate attempt to use the Christian faith for the construction of a system of knowledge. By its complicated cosmologies, Gnosticism sought to provide a Christian solution to problems like the origin of evil, which had engaged the best minds of classical antiquity. It thus claimed to provide its adherents with a new and higher type of knowledge, denied to those who had not been admitted to its esoteric circle. In keeping with its claim to higher knowledge, Gnosticism tried to distinguish various levels of knowledge within the Bible as well as within the church; hence *Marcion's* repudiation of the Old Testament and his revision of the New Testament.[1]

The orthodox rejection of the Gnostic tendency has tended to obscure the fact that a number of its emphases found their way into the body of Christian teaching.[2] Clement of Alexandria and Origen earned the name "Christian Gnostics," and the apologists and early fathers joined in asserting that Christianity was a new and celestial philosophy.[3] The secrecy surrounding the Christian creed, the discipline that granted Christian truth only to the faithful, and the competition of Christianity with classical thought all helped to give the impression that being a Christian meant knowing certain truths and being able to recite them in the correct and traditional manner. It is a matter of interpretation whether we term this development an acute Hellenization of Christianity, as did Adolf Harnack, or whether we regard it as a deft synthesis of the Greek and the Christian view. Nygren has seen the epitome of this synthesis in Augustine's concept of *caritas* so far as the understanding of love was concerned, but there was a similar synthesis of Greek and Christian thought in the interpretation of truth. Plato had taught that God was truth, as he had taught that God was love. In both cases, many of the fathers invested Christian terms

---

[1] Cf. John Knox, *Marcion and the New Testament* (Chicago, 1942) for a careful interpretation.

[2] James Thomas Carlyon, "The Impact of Gnosticism on Early Christianity" in J. T. McNeill (ed.), *Environmental Factors in Christian History* (Chicago, 1939), pp. 114-130.

[3] See Charles Norris Cochrane's delineation of "Nostra Philosophia," Ch. XI of his *Christianity and Classical Culture* (London, 1940), pp. 399-455.

with Greek meanings and thus produced a synthesis which interpreted love as desire for self-realization, and knowledge as intellectual mastery over given truth.[4]

In the thought of Origen, and more particularly in the theology of St. Augustine, this synthesis gave Christianity the intellectual respectability that the Greco-Roman world demanded in any system of thought. With the closer integration of Christianity into Western culture, such intellectual respectability became the mark of a theology which sought to conquer all the areas of thought for its central convictions and affirmations. Parallel with the increasing domination of the church over secular life was the growing control which theology came to exercise over the intellect and its operations. The climax of both developments came during the thirteenth century, when Pope Innocent III ruled as the arbiter of Europe and Thomas Aquinas welded a system of thought in which philosophy, education, art, science, and politics were co-ordinated by being subordinated to theology, or, as he himself termed it, "sacred science." This sacred science differed from the other sciences in that its transmitter was the Holy Spirit, who had blessed it with an absoluteness which the others could not have. By virtue of that absoluteness, sacred science could criticize all the discoveries and claims of other fields of thought and suffer ultimate criticism from none of them, just as the pope was to judge all but be judged by none.

------

[4] Anders Nygren, *Agape and Eros*, trans. by Philip S. Watson (2nd ed.; Philadelphia, 1953), pp. 515 ff. on the relation of *caritas* and speculation.

As theology gradually became a sacred science committed to the church's trust, the church began to think
of itself as the repository of divine truth and of its
mission in history as the communication of this truth to
ignorant mankind. For the uneducated, the medieval
church had the seven sacraments, and in addition relics
and sacramentals. For those who could read and think,
the church provided a divine truth, worked up into a
system that permitted the exercise of the highest speculative gifts of the metaphysical mind. In spite of the
frantic assertion that there was no qualitative difference
between the faith of the old woman in the garden and
the faith of the philosopher-theologian, the fact remains that by developing these systems the church
laid such a stress upon the intellectual apprehension of
Christian truth as to give the impression that God had
endowed the doctors of the church with a special gift
of His grace enabling them to penetrate into mysteries
that were hidden to the uninitiated, uneducated eyes
of the simpler folk.[5] In a sense, then, metaphysics had
become a means of grace.

Because that impression was current in the medieval
church, Luther and the Reformers singled it out as one
of the chief targets in their critique of Roman Catholicism. For example, the Augsburg Confession and its
Apology denied that "historical faith," a knowledge of
the facts and dogmas of the Christian faith, could ever
save a man. Knowing the history of Christ was not

---

[5]On the doctrine of the *vetula*, cf. the discussion of Etienne Gilson, *Christianity and Philosophy*, trans. by Ralph McDonald (New York, 1939), pp. 57-58.

enough, one had to know Christ himself. To know
Christ was to know His blessings.[6] This judgment could
have eliminated the identification of the Holy and the
True from Christian theology. But the very Protestantism
which began by decrying that identification in medieval
scholasticism eventually developed its own scholasticism and with it a renewed attempt to define faith as
intellectual assent, and revelation as the transmission
of sacred truths.

This happened in both the Reformed and the Lutheran families. The phenomenon which one interpreter
has termed "the Melanchthonian blight" in Lutheran
theology,[7] was the notion that agreement to a set of
intellectual propositions was the constitutive factor in
faith. In both the Lutheran and the Reformed churches,
the pulpit gradually became a dogmatic lecture-plat-
form and the voice of the theological systematician
carried the tune in the choir immortal. The great com-
mission to make disciples of all nations gave theologians an excuse to compose intricate metaphysical
systems and to indoctrinate clergy and laity by making
conformity to those systems a prerequisite for membership in the church.

Having entrenched itself in the church once more
through its endorsement by later Protestantism, intellectualism remained even after Orthodox Protestantism
had withered away. The Rationalism that took over

---

[6]Jaroslav Pelikan, "The Origins of the Object-Subject Antithesis in
Lutheran Dogmatics," *Concordia Theological Monthly,* XXI (1950),
94-104.

[7]Richard R. Caemmerer, "The Melanchthonian Blight," *ibid.,*
XVIII (1947), 321-338.

the ideological leadership of Protestantism in the eighteenth century appeared in the same intellectualist guise that had clothed the older systems. By a curious transfer which is not unique in the history of thought, the Enlightenment continued to equate the Holy and the True, even though it did not share Orthodoxy's definition of the specific True with which the Holy was to be equated.[8] Insisting as it did upon intellectual apprehension and rational demonstration as the essential elements of Christian faith and witness, late seventeenth-century Protestant theology dropped its guard to any system of thought which found that such intellectual apprehension and rational demonstration produced conclusions contrary to orthodox theology. Before the danger of such an insistence had become evident, Rationalism had managed to call most of Orthodoxy's tenets into question, and to do so on the basis of Orthodoxy's own identification of the Holy and the True. So long as that identification stood, Orthodoxy fought against Rationalism with blunt weapons, for even when the True was thought of as divine in origin and communication, this led to a barren intellectualism in which faith faded away amid the claims and counterclaims of competing metaphysical systems.

The intellectualism which so much of the history of theology had maintained produced its own destroyer in Immanuel Kant. It was his abiding achieve-

---

[8]Ernst Cassirer, *The Philosophy of the Enlightenment*, trans. by Fritz A. C. Koelln and James P. Pettegrove (Princeton, 1951), pp. 3-36, and *passim*.

ment to subvert the foundations upon which the
identification of the Holy and the True had been built,
making such an identification impossible for anyone
who took his critiques seriously. As we shall see, Kant
disposed of one error only to fall into another, he
rejected intellectualism to embrace moralism. More
significant in the present context is the fact that in
spite of the deathblow which Kant dealt to intellectualism at the close of the eighteenth century, there were
still many who fell right back into the intellectualist
pattern. Though they claimed to be taking up where
Kant had left off, these thinkers actually suppressed
the deepest implications of Kant's critical philosophy.
As a matter of fact, the identification of the Holy and
the True was as strong in the nineteenth century as it
had ever been.[9]

Symbolic of that fact is the thought of Hegel and
of the Hegelian theologians. By the time his long and
tortuous development was completed, Hegel had
evolved a system that rivaled scholasticism for compre-
hensiveness and intricacy. In this system the identification of the Holy and the True was very explicit:
God was the reasoning Spirit of the universe, and the
worship of God consisted in thinking His thoughts after
Him as accurately as possible. Taking their cue from
this notion of God, the Hegelian theologians came to
describe the Christian God in the same terms. Whatever may be its validity otherwise, Hegelian metaphysics certainly succeeded in distorting the Christian

---

[9]Cf. Karl Barth, *Die protestantische Theologie im 19. Jahrhundert*
(Zurich, 1947), pp. 374 ff. on Hegel's concept of the True.

picture of God, until the intellectualism which had been at work throughout the history of theology came to fruition in the theological formulations that Kierkegaard scornfully dubbed "the System."

When Kierkegaard appeared on the scene, therefore, nineteenth-century thought, both philosophical and theological, had begun once more to equate the Holy and the True and to regard faith and knowledge as synonymous. As we have seen, it could claim a long and distinguished ancestry for such a point of view. From the prominence of the identification of the Holy and the True in ancient, medieval, and modern thought, it would seem to be endowed with a certain allure that has continued to draw theologians and philosophers. There are, in fact, several elements that have made it tempting to any thinker whose task it was to formulate and expound Christian teachings in a systematic way.

It is noteworthy that this identification has appeared most frequently among those thinkers who have employed the affirmations of the Christian faith in the construction of comprehensive and intellectually validated systems. There can be no denying the importance for the cultured and sophisticated of an integrated and symmetrical world view, a system by which the claims and discoveries of the several fields of human endeavor could be balanced and harmonized in a higher synthesis. The mind has refused to surrender its dream of such a synthesis and to content itself with a fragmentary world view. In William James's terms, it has continually sought to change the *each*-form, where it knew only some things, into an *all*-form, where it knew all things and related them to each other in such a way that they seemed to form a harmonious and unified whole.[10] Like Faust, the educated mind has yearned for a systematic interpretation of all the phenomena of experience, informed by one central idea.

When the central idea animating a man's thought and life has been the Christian faith, it is to Christian theology that he has turned to provide the context for his system. The systems developed by men like Thomas Aquinas have testified to the resources within Christian theology for the construction of such a synthesis. Likewise, the loyal support which Thomism has evoked among many of our contemporaries suggests how various Christian philosophies have been able to compete on even terms with secular metaphysics. The central teachings of the Christian faith about God, man, and the world have been the raw material for a number of well-rounded and self-contained systems.

Because Christian philosophy has thus shown its capacity to meet the demand for integration and symmetry characteristic of the natural mind, the systematizers of Christian theology have often been tempted to employ Christian convictions in such a way as to answer that demand. This has certainly been a chief source of the identification of the Holy and the True in Christian thought. In using the resources of theology for the purposes of philosophy, Christian thinkers have tended to make a philosophy out of their theology, thus equating the Holy (the traditional sub-

---

[10]William James, A *Pluralistic Universe* (New York, 1943), p. 34.

ject of religious discourse) and the True (the traditional province of philosophical, specifically of metaphysical analysis).

Closely connected with this tendency to make of Christianity an intellectually validated metaphysical system is the danger implicit in any systematic articulation of the Christian faith. Such systematic articulations have become necessary because of a number of considerations. Since the first century, the church has responded to challenges inside as well as outside its membership by drawing up statements of faith or confessions. Similar statements were called for in the Christian nurture which the church provided for its catechumens. The training of the clergy required the preparation of theological texts to make clear the church's position on the important questions of Christian thought. Only the most extreme of critics would suggest that in facing up to these needs the church made a mistake when it composed systematic and thorough expositions of Christian doctrine. For the continuity of its teaching and confession, the church has certainly needed such expositions in the past and will continue to need them in the future.

For just that reason, however, systematic theologians have constantly run the risk of making the identification we have been discussing. It is more than coincidence that it has been most frequent among them. Since there is no other satisfactory medium of communication for Christian doctrine, the church's articulation of the gospel has been verbal, and by the nature of the needs which called it forth, that articulation usually has assumed a formal character. It is to the development of these verbal, formal articulations of the gospel that theologians have devoted themselves, and it is around these articulations that theological controversies have usually centered. Theological polemic, then, has often consisted in a defense of these articulations, rather than of the gospel as such, even though the theologian maintained that he was defending the gospel for which the articulations stood. There are few confusions more subtle or more dangerous than that of symbol and reality. The use of the word "symbol" as a synonym for "confession" suggests that articulations of the gospel are signs to mark and identify the teaching of the gospel. They are surely that, but they are not therefore to be confused with the gospel itself. Systematic theologians have frequently been led by their distinctive task and responsibility to make this unfortunate confusion. When they have done so and have identified the gospel with theology, they have fallen into the identification of the Holy and the True, which has been the peculiar propensity and the occupational disease of those charged with the teaching of systematic theology.

As has already been mentioned, the identification of the Holy and the True is part of our Greek heritage. This identification was part of one of the fundamental fallacies in Greek philosophy, the equation of knowledge and virtue in the teaching of Socrates. As one form of the natural yearning for a valid and integrated system, this equation has made the quest for knowledge and certainty central in all of life, just as the reason was the central feature in the human personality. It demanded information about the external world and about ultimate truth, and it believed that such information was sufficient to develop valid maxims for human life and conduct. In short, it believed that knowledge saved.

To the extent that Christian thought has fallen into this fallacy of equating knowledge and virtue, it has thereby committed the error of identifying the Holy and the True. It has assumed that a knowledge of certain truths about God provided the knower with a relationship to God he could not otherwise secure, and has made the inculcation of such knowledge its principal aim and purpose. What it has added to the Greek view in such an instance is a more ambitious claim to absoluteness and intellectual certainty than Greek thought had felt able to make, but this deepened its involvement in the identification of the Holy and the True rather than alleviating it. By permitting itself to lay claim to absolutely reliable intellectual knowledge, it has often become more guilty of the *hybris* in Greek philosophy than that philosophy itself had been.

What the Greek saw as *hybris*, unseemly and rapacions seizure, Christian thought diagnosed as sin, as the attempt to rule God instead of being ruled by Him. This seems to have been the most basic allurement of the identification of the Holy and the True, underlying and preceding all others. It was the desire to make of God an object of my knowing and my thinking, the highest object to be sure, but still one object among other objects over which I could assume mastery by learning to know them. Knowledge was power, and knowledge of God was power over God. By learning the right things about God, one was initiated into the secrets of His being and could call upon one's knowledge of those secrets for aid in the solution of life's problems. Just as the doctrine of the analogy of being saw God as one being among the entire series of beings making up the universe, so the doctrine of the objective knowledge of God brought God into the realm of the infinite number of objects making up the body of human knowledge.

If one could succeed in relegating God to this status as an object of experience and knowledge, one automatically deprived Him of His status as subject, as the Thou who had "searched me and known me," as the Lord whom man could not control as Aladdin summoued the genie of the lamp. It would be his fondest hope to get rid of the disquieting and judging knowledge by God through the interjection of a knowledge about God. Objective knowledge one could control, and thus master the doctrines of systematic theology by learning them. What comfort and security there would be in the human mind if it could dispose of God's penetrating and judging look by subjecting the Holy, whose wrath it can neither tolerate nor dominate, to the True, with which it can live on reasonably satisfactory terms. Here has been the most profound source of the equation of the Holy and the True, as well as the factor that has made it a manifestation of sin.

To Soren Kierkegaard must go the distinction of having penetrated more deeply than any other Chris-

tian thinker, at least since Luther, into the subtle fallacy
of identifying the Holy and the True.[11] There had been
other criticisms of that identification before him. The
philosophy of Kant and the religiousness of Pietism
were both directed against intellectualism. In his
critique of the intellectualist heresy Kierkegaard included many of the principal elements in the previous
analyses and added his own distinctive emphases. Our
discussion of his attacks upon the identification of the
Holy and True will examine both the criticism he
shared with other opponents of intellectualism and the
unique judgments which he added to that criticism.

Like the Pietism with which he displayed some interesting affinities, Kierkegaard repeatedly made the
charge that an overemphasis upon the intellectual
apprehension of Christian truth often brought on a
corresponding decline in the ethical consciousness of
the church.[12] Pietism had been brought to this conviction by the example of late Orthodox Protestantism,
which almost seemed to tolerate every sin but heresy.
Kierkegaard experienced a similar phenomenon in the
Danish church of his time, whose leaders sometimes
seemed to pay more attention to the theological implications of Hegelian metaphysics than to the ethical
implications of Christian theology.

[11]See the brief discussion of David Swenson, "Kierkegaard's Anti-
Intellectualism," *Something about Kierkegaard* (Minneapolis, 1941),
pp. 95-118. A very moving presentation of Kierkegaard's thought is
the essay of Melville Chaning-Pearce, "Kierkegaard" in Donald Att-
water (ed.), *Modern Christian Revolutionaries* (New York, 1947),
pp. 3-85.
[12]*Attack upon "Christendom,"* trans. by Walter Lowrie (Princeton,
1944), pp. 259 ff. on how the priests have demoralized Christendom.

Though this may not have been the most profound refutation of intellectualism, it was certainly a valid one. It was not the most profound because moralism was not the Christian antidote to intellectualism (we shall devote ourselves to this issue later). As far as it went, the criticism was well taken. The acceptance of information about God as true did often become a means of defense against the imperatives of the Christian ethic. Doctrinal correctness was no sure indication of a truly Christian life. According to the theologians, sanctification was supposed to follow upon justification, yet it did not always do so—particularly not when justification by faith was rooted in an understanding of faith that defined it as knowledge and assent. On this count, the identification of the Holy and the True was open to criticism, and very serious criticism at that.

Intellectualism fled from the demands of Christian ethics by fixing the locus of faith in the intellect rather than in the will. In keeping with this, it interpreted the certainty of faith and the assurance of salvation intellectually, and thus was compelled to predicate an absolute certainty of the propositions to which it held. When the Christian knowledge of God was cast in the framework of the object-subject antithesis,[13] the objective knowledge of God that it required brought with it an unwarranted assumption about the absolute character of a particular theological knowledge. Intellectualism often led to dogmatism. Like David Hume and

---

[13]See note 6 above; also Rudolf Eucken, *Main Currents of Modern Thought*, trans. by Meyrick Booth (New York, 1912), pp. 35-63.

Immanuel Kant before him, Kierkegaard protested against intellectualism on this ground, too.[14]

By "the System,"[15] Kierkegaard meant to convey his contempt for the pretensions of a dogmatism that claimed to have encased the truth in an airtight compartment from which truth could never escape. Truth was not something that could be manipulated at will, controlled or mastered. Hume and Kant arrived at their critiques of intellectualism by a rather calm analysis of the capacities and potentialities of the reason for coping with the data of sense-experience and by the isolation of the a priori that preceded sense-experience. As the existential thinker that he was, Kierkegaard was incapable of any such dispassionate analysis. Kant's answer to intellectualism was itself a superb example of the intellect's proclivity for abstract thought, but Kierkegaard objected to abstraction as such. In abstract thought he saw a subtle attempt by the mind to rob truth of its existential judgment upon the total ego. By developing into "the System" a truth which had addressed the individual in personal and existential encounter, the Hegelians had managed to disarm truth and render it harmless. Such a course had permitted them to find an unjustified security and an objective certainty in a truth thus deprived of its personal quality. After all, being mistaken was not the worst possible fate that could befall a theologian.

---

[14]"The Absolute Paradox: A Metaphysical Crotchet," *Philosophical Fragments*, trans. by David Swenson (Princeton, 1946), pp. 29-38.

[15]On the "System," cf., for example, the discussion of Lessing in *Concluding Unscientific Postscript*, trans. by David Swenson and Walter Lowrie (Princeton, 1941), pp. 97 ff.

Alongside these two objections to intellectualism, on the grounds that it stultified morality and that it bred an arrogant dogmatism, Kierkegaard also voiced a third criticism—that truth could often come in other ways than through the intellect. In an age dominated as much as the past two centuries have been by science and the scientific method, those who fear mechanism have turned for support to the poets and artists. Professor Whitehead suggested that the metaphysicians of the future may be its poets rather than its philosophers, and that more than once, as in the case of Plato, this had been true of the past as well.[16]

Some of the problems connected with this suggestion will concern us later, when we examine the values and the inadequacies of aestheticism as a categorization of the Holy. In Kierkegaard's century, the opposition to the primacy of intellect as the medium for acquiring knowledge came especially from the Romantic school of writers and thinkers in Germany, France, and England. Realizing that scientific mechanism would bring on what Nietzsche termed "the devaluation of all values," the Romantics demanded the recognition that poetry communicated a higher knowledge than did prose, and that there was a wisdom in the history of the race which the intellect could neither transmit nor judge.

That point of view came to frequent expression in the writings of Kierkegaard, amid many other traces of his Romantic leanings. Now and again he spoke

---

[16]Alfred North Whitehead, *Modes of Thought* (New York, 1938), pp. 237-238.

highly of "poesy" as a means for learning truth which
the apostles of "the System" had ignored.[17] In fact, his
own writings were an exhibit of the thesis that the most
profound expositions of wisdom and knowledge do not
come in balanced, symmetrical presentations, but in
occasional flashes of insight and intuition at which the
plodding and ponderous reason could never arrive. In
form as well as in content, some of Kierkegaard's best
writing was sheer poetry, lyric in its delicacy and grace,
epic in the sweep and grandeur of its conceptions and
imagery. He has therefore been called a "poet of
faith."

None of these criticisms, however, represents either
the most distinctive or the most penetrating attack
that Kierkegaard made upon intellectualism. All of
these were either ethical, epistemological, or aesthetic,
while Kierkegaard was at his best as a religious prophet.
If the identification of the Holy and the True was to be
judged, it had ultimately to be judged from the standpoint of faith. Analyses and evaluations of it that treated
its interpretation of the True may have been valuable,
but what finally had to decide the case for or against
it was what it did to the Holy. It was on this score that
Kierkegaard's critique of intellectualism was most significant, and on this score that he finally rejected the
identification not merely on ethical or epistemological
or aesthetic grounds, but in the name of the Christian
gospel.

One of the principal errors involved in the heresy of
intellectualism, according to Kierkegaard, was what

---

[17]Chaning-Pearce, op. cit., pp. 36-38.

we might term its doctrine of prevenient grace. Intellectualism was founded on the proposition that the acquisition of a given amount of religious knowledge was prerequisite to the establishment of fellowship between God and man. It depended upon the theory that God's self-disclosure could be won by the mastery of a quantum of information about God, and that native intelligence or education or rational competence would call forth God's revelation. As a corollary it would maintain that where intelligence, training, or rationality were lacking, God most certainly would not reveal himself.

Christianity made the opposite claim. It asserted that not many wise or educated or rational men would be able to accept the foolishness of the preaching of the gospel, and it despaired of the attempt to lead men through reason to faith.[18] No amount of training or knowledge or ratiocination would cause faith to rise "with lubricated ease," as Professor Sittler has put it, out of the natural mind.[19] Intellectualism erred in supposing that a mind supplied with truths about God therefore had faith. Having equated the Holy and the True, it interpreted faith as intellectual assent to the

---

[18]"Christianity teaches that everything Christian exists only for faith; for this reason precisely it wills to be a Socratic, a Godfearing ignorance, which by ignorance defends the faith against speculation, keeping watch to see that the deep gulf of qualitative distinction between God and man may be finally fixed, as it is in the paradox and in faith, lest God and man, still more dreadfully than ever it occurred in paganism, might in a way, *philosophice, poetice* etc., coalesce into one . . . in the System." *Sickness unto Death*, trans. by Walter Lowrie (Princeton, 1944), p. 161.

[19]Joseph Sittler, *The Doctrine of the Word in the Structure of Lutheran Theology* (Philadelphia, 1948), p. 35.

True and as agreement with an external authority. But
God had chosen the simple of the earth to confound
the wise, had most unreasonably made himself known
in the Incarnation to shatter the pretensions of the
philosophers. While the philosophy of Athens and the
theology of Jerusalem were speculating about Him, He
chose to be born in Bethlehem, to the utter consterna-
tion of both speculative philosophy and theology ever
since.

With these and similar thoughts Kierkegaard made
known his passionate opposition to the identification
of the Holy and the True on the grounds that it laid
down conditions to God without which He dared not
reveal himself. Here, too, belong the unkind things he
had to say about professors of theology, who had rationalized the Christian paradox.[20] Theology was
neither the event of God in Christ, nor a witness to
that event. It was merely a description of the witness
to the event, and a professor of systematic theology
was in the lamentable position of being a professor of
the description of the witness to the event, thus several
stages removed from the event itself. He contrasted
this with the faith of the apostles, much to the dis-
advantage of the theological "genius" who would wish
by his system to replace the vigor and power of the

---

[20]Cf. *Postscript*, p. 198: "When Christianity came into the world
there were no professors and *Privatdocents* at all; then it was a paradox for everyone. In the present generation it may be assumed that
one out of every ten is a *Privatdocent*; hence Christianity is a paradox
for nine out of ten. And when finally the fullness of time arrived, that
extraordinary future when an entire generation of male and female
Privatdocents peoples the earth, then Christianity will have ceased
to be a paradox."

apostolic witness with a set of intellectual propositions.[21]

, Not only was revelation a free act of God's will
called forth by His grace rather than by men's wisdom.
Even when it did come, it did not consist primarily in
the transmission of truths or of information, but in the
establishment of a fellowship. Kierkegaard's *Concluding Unscientific Postscript* was devoted to an exposition
of this teaching. Revelation was personal, it was not
conceptual. Intellectual capacity was no criterion for
revelation, not only because God revealed himself to
the simple, but also because the revelation He did
confer was not intellectually apprehended. Indeed, it
was not apprehended at all. It was man who was apprehended, seized, taken captive by the Holy One who
addressed him in Christ Jesus. God was not an object
among other objects which man could control through
his knowledge, and relationship to Him was not a
matter of objective data which man added to the
storehouse of information he had accumulated.[22]

In the phrase "knowledge of God," then, the term
'God" was primarily subjective rather than objective
genitive. Knowledge of God was knowledge by God
before becoming knowledge about God. Man's knowledge of God was the personal communion into which
God called him by knowing him in Christ. Such knowl-

---

[21]"One is to suffer; the other is to become a professor of the fact that
another has suffered." *Journals*, ed. and trans. by Alexander Dru
Oxford, 1938), No. 1362.

[22]"If I am capable of grasping God objectively, I do not believe,
but precisely because I cannot do this I must believe." *Postscript*,
. 182.

edge did not stand in continuity with the intellectual
apprehension received in science and philosophy. This
was the deepest meaning of Kierkegaard's famous statement in the *Postscript* and elsewhere that "truth is
subjectivity."[23] Christian truth was subjective not in
the sense that the individual's subjective judgment de-
cided what was true and what was not, but in the
sense that all standards and criteria of objective knowledge collapsed before the Holy, for the mind could
not enclose or grasp Him. In other forms of knowledge,
the initiative might come from the inquiring and investigating mind; but in the knowledge communicated
by revelation, the initiative was of God, who disclosed
His fatherly heart to give himself by re-establishing
His fellowship. When the mind sought to create proofs
of Him or propositions about Him in which it could
believe, He stopped being the Thou of faith and became merely an It. Then there was no more revelation.
For once the Holy had become an object of intellectual
apprehension, and faith in Him the acceptance of
propositions about Him, the relation between God and
man had left the personal, existential dimension within
which alone revelation and faith had any meaning.

Since the revelation of God was a personal revelation
and since it was intended to call man into fellowship
with God, it followed that the responsibility which the
conferring of that revelation involved was personal
too. At first glance, this insight of Kierkegaard's might
sound like an ethical judgment; it was not primarily
that. Responsibility was more than duty or ethical

---

[23]*Ibid.*, pp. 169-224.

requirement. It was the "Yes" which my total being offered to God's "Yes" in Christ, it was my part in the fellowship which revelation created. No mere ethical judgment this, as though God had torn me loose from my moorings and uprooted my very life just in order to make me good. This was the response which my total being gave to the Holy One, to Him who draws me and yet I know can destroy me, to Him whom I can neither understand nor comprehend and yet without whom I cannot live.[24]

Confronted by God's call and brought by His Spirit to such a response, how could I try to use the little systems of my mind as devices to win His favor?[25] Having once learned to know existentially the impact of the Holy, I had to surrender all hope of defining Him or, as Kierkegaard put it, of having someone tell me about Him while I am shaving. The identification of the Holy and the True completely ignored the fact that there could be no definition and no argument when God was present, and that the Christian faith was concerned with the relation of the Holy to me, not with the relation of information to my mind.

This existential and religious repudiation of the identification of the Holy and the True was the root of what is often called Kierkegaard's "anti-intellectualism."

---

[24]On proof and doubt, cf. *Edifying Discourses,* trans. by David Swenson and Lillian Swenson, II (Minneapolis, 1944), 38-39. On Kierkegaard's interpretation of the faith-response, see the contrast of the tragic hero and the knight of faith, *Fear and Trembling,* trans. by Walter Lowrie (Princeton, 1945), pp. 102-123.

[25]Cf. Kierkegaard's stirring discussion of "being alone with God's Word," *For Self-Examination,* trans. by Walter Lowrie (London, 1941), pp. 55 ff.

As Karl Holl has pointed out, much harm has come
from careless talk about irrationalism and anti-intellectualism.[26] If Kierkegaard, like Luther, was suspicious
of the possibilities of the reason for knowing God and
coming to terms with Him, this was not, as Gilson and
others have claimed, a desire to wound nature in order
to magnify grace.[27] In response to such a claim Kierkegaard would have asserted that his antagonists had
not yet learned to exist! To attempt to juggle the
claims of nature versus grace or of reason versus revelation or of philosophy versus theology in the presence
of the living God was, in Kierkegaard's judgment, an
example of how the intellect sought to divert God from
His attack upon the individual's pride and his very life.

Nor can Kierkegaard's answer to intellectualism be
dismissed by calling it irrationalism, fideism, or theologism. For one thing, it was not any of these as they are
usually defined. Even if it had been, that would not
change the fact that no one who takes Kierkegaard
seriously dare ever try to use any system—and this includes Kierkegaard's system!—as a screen of truth to
keep God out, or to create a theology to which God
must accommodate himself or perish.

This is what Kierkegaard finally perceived in the
clear light of his madness. His madness permitted him

---

[26] Karl Holl, "Was verstand Luther unter Religion?", *Gesammelte
Aufsaetze zur Kirchengeschichte*, I, *Luther* (7th ed.; Tuebingen,
1948), 35-36, note 3.
[27] Etienne Gilson, "Nature and Philosophy," *Christianity and Philosophy*, pp. 1-26; also his *L'esprit de la philosophie medievale* (2nd
ed.; Paris, 1944), p. 399. "A speculative philosopher is finished on
paper, and confuses this with existence." *Postscript*, p. 406.

to see, more clearly than most, the blasphemy of identifying the Holy and the True, and he was able to face
up to it with a consistency and a rigor that only the
mad or the half-mad can afford. He had been brought
up in a tradition that promised absolute intellectual
assurance to its adherents. The theology which he
studied asserted that such assurance was God's means
of granting the certainty of salvation. To this was
added a Hegelianism that was, if anything, more ex-
travagant in its claims. All the phenomena of nature
and of history, the ego and God and the world, were
brought together in Hegel's system into one comprehensive world view. Such was the background out of
which Kierkegaard came, and from it he learned to
expect and to demand objective intellectual certainty
of any system of thought that presented itself to him
for judgment.

All the more terrifying was it, therefore, to discover
that in dealing with the Holy there was no guarantee
of such certainty, indeed, that such certainty was impossible and even hostile to the true knowledge of God.
The Greek mind, the philosophical mind in general,
regarded insistence upon objective certainty and intellectual assurance as a legitimate criterion for the validity of an idea. When the Christian faith tried to
establish its validity before the judgment of the Greek
mind, it found it easy to transfer that certainty which
was given in the fellowship of the Holy Spirit through
the Word into the realm of the intellect and, by rational
proofs and elaborate demonstrations, to show that
Christianity did not have to bow to any philosophical

system in the intellectual assurance it could offer.
Hence the identification of the Holy and the True,
which has dominated entire centuries of theological
history.

Precisely because this has been so common a phenomenon in the history of theology and philosophy and
because it has provided its supporters with magnificent
systems of thought, the equation of the Holy and the
True has been such a dangerous and insidious heresy.
And it took a madman who did not have to care about
consequences to make that danger clear. This is what
makes Kierkegaard the madman a "fool for Christ,"
that he used his madness in the service of God and
thereby brought theologians a lesson which their less
eccentric teachers could never have taught them so
graphically.

The lesson is not an easy one to learn. It involves
a deep penance, for the habits of centuries are not
lightly brushed aside. Theology has flirted with being
a philosophy so long and so successfully that theologians find it hard to admit that the Holy and the
True are not the same. But Kierkegaard's realization
that the Holy cannot and dare not be identified with
the True is a necessary prerequisite for thought and
work in systematic theology. Without a deep and existential consciousness of this, systematic theology will
try again and again, in Luther's terms, to be a *theologia
gloriae* instead of a *theologia crucis*,[28] a metaphysical
system of speculation instead of a biblical testimony to
the Cross. For the task of Christian theology is to de-

---

[28]Nygren, *op. cit.*, pp. 700 ff.

scribe, afterwards, what God has done in Christ, and to do so in faith's own terms. When it seeks to elevate itself into a higher metaphysic or some sacred or sacral science, it betrays and destroys itself.

In this essay we have dealt only with the first problem of systematic theology, namely, the impossibility of thinking from the True to the Holy. In the next essay we shall consider the second and more constructive problem of theological method, namely, the necessity of thinking from the Holy to the True. To deal with that problem adequately we have first had to venture, with Soren Kierkegaard, through and beyond our feebly constructed systems, into the dread and the fascination that came to him in those moments when he knew the madness of the Holy.

PAUL

The question of the relationship between the Holy
and the True was an active issue in the thought of
Paul's time, and one to which some of the best minds of
the period were devoting their attention. In the classical
world the concept of truth was a central area of concern; and in Paul's more immediate surroundings, in
Hellenistic and Palestinian Judaism, sages and savants
had developed a thoroughgoing idea of the meaning
of truth. Among both Greeks and Jews, the estimate of
the True was high enough to warrant our saying that
for both truth had become a sort of Christ, so that they
did not accept the truth in Christ because they had
found a Christ in truth.

One of the fundamental problems in Greek metaphysics was put by Aristotle in three precise mono-
syllables: *ti to on?* What does it mean "to be"? The
quest for the precise nature of being dominated Greek
philosophy throughout the schools, and it came ultimately to determine the picture of God as well. For
above the gods of the mythologies, even above fate,
the discerning eye of the wisest Greeks came to behold

pure, disembodied being itself, a being that was no longer caught in the mutability of becoming and potentiality but was pure actuality, the *actus purus*. This disembodied being had some affinity with mortal man in that man, too, "is." Thus in a sense, man and God were linked together in what Lovejoy has happily termed "the great chain of being."[1] Man had only to be brought to the point where he could realize this affinity of his "being."

He did this by truth. Whether it came by an anamnesis or recollection of what he had always carried within the shrine of his heart, as Plato believed, or whether it came from without, truth was a means of grace, or at least a means of being, a channel for the human mind to gain that vision of God as being which made man's life meaningful and blessed. The efforts of the Greek mind to gain this truth were little short of prodigious. The Book of Acts tells us that fully four centuries after the death of Plato all the men of Athens "spent their time in nothing except telling or hearing something new." Even these curiosity-seekers exemplified the Greek pursuit of truth, even their flirtation with truth breathed the Greek passion for this goddess whose beauty they desired as the hart panteth after the water brooks. There was no explicit messianism in Greek philosophy partly, at least, because truth held a place in Greek thought that Christ was to hold in Christian thought— the revelation of the Most High. If the Most High was thought of as being, then the revelation could be thought of as truth. Acquisition of truth, growth in

---

[1] Arthur O. Lovejoy, *The Great Chain of Being* (Cambridge, 1936).

knowledge, and cultivation of the reason could thus become religious virtues. For the Greek, then, truth was a matter of prime importance as a means for coming into contact and ultimately into union with being itself.[2]

⌐ For the Jew of Paul's time, too, truth was a treasure highly to be prized. If the Greeks spent their time seeking it and rejoicing over pieces of it that they found, the Jews devoted themselves to cultivating a truth that needed no seeking any longer⌐ As a chosen people, they were in possession of it forever. So aware were they of their superiority to lesser breeds without the law that they had also made truth into a kind of Christ: still expecting the redemption of God to come out of Zion and therefore anticipating a further intervention of God in the life and history of His people; but secure meanwhile in their knowledge of just what form that intervention would take, where and how the Anointed of God would arise. They speculated on the coming of the Christ, and they associated certain signs with that coming. But of this they were sure, that whatever truth he would bring would merely substantiate or at best supplement the truth they had, but would in no way revise or replace it. The Christ would come to fulfil the truth they already had, he would confirm the correctness of the truth they had known all along. Any Christ

---

[2]Cf. Werner Jaeger, Paideia: The Ideals of Greek Culture, trans. by Gilbert Highet (3 vols.; New York, 1945), I, 178: "It was the consciousness of his high mission which led him, in the prelude to his poem [Parmenides on aletheia], to draw the first real picture of a philosopher—the 'man who knows,' led by the daughters of light, far from the paths of men, along the hard road to the house of truth."

who did not match that truth was a false Messiah, a blasphemer elevating himself over their father Abraham and their teacher Moses, undermining the truth and subverting the law. "We have a law, and by that law he ought to die."

The law was truth. Unfortunately, the English word "law" carries primarily classical and juridical connotations and seems to imply principally or even exclusively a code of moral demands. To the Jew it was this also, to be sure, but *torah* had a far broader meaning, as even a cursory examination of the Psalms will show.[8] It meant instruction, teaching, and would often be well rendered by the English word "doctrine." A study of the equivalent Greek term *nomos* in the Septuagint and in Philo seems to show that this more inclusive significance attached to the term in post-biblical and even in Hellenistic Judaism. Blended as it was in Hellenistic Judiasm with the Platonic view of *nomos* and the Greek view of truth, the law came to be equated with truth, codified or written revelation. Already in the Old Testament it was one of the most frequent designations for the written form of the Word of God. It was the Jew's exclusive possession, with which all other "truth" had to be brought into some sort of harmony. He who knew the law and performed it would live before God. This was the *nomos*-motif, as Nygren terms it—a concept to which he seems to devote

---

[8] On the meaning of *torah* in the Psalms and other sections of the Old Testament, cf. Walter Gutbrod, *s.v.* "nomos" in Gerhard Kittel (ed.), *Theologisches Woerterbuch zum Neuen Testament* (Stuttgart, 1933 ff.), IV, 1029-1040; on Philo, pp. 1044-1046.

less attention than it deserves.[4] Filled with the realization that to them and to them alone this *torah*-truth had been entrusted, many Jews of Paul's day earnestly desired to instruct the nations and to give them a truth they could not learn in any other way. Awareness of possessing the truth formed a powerful impulse to a missionary effort among the Jews in the Empire. The evolution of the synagogue also helped to confirm them in their truth.[5]

Into this world—where Greeks prized truth and sought it, and Jews prized truth and possessed it—came one who was debtor to them both, but a slave of Jesus Christ: Paul the apostle. With skills of dissection worthy of the finest surgeons or coroners, New Testament scholars in the past century and a half have analyzed the writings of Paul with a view toward isolating in them those ideas and terms which he owed to either Gentile or Jewish sources. They have not always kept sight of the fact that, while a debtor to both, he transcended them and transmuted them as an apostle of his risen Lord. Tempted though he may have been to find a Christ in truth, that is, to find the ultimate fulfilment of his existence in the possession of Greek wisdom or Jewish revelation, he nevertheless

---

[4]Nygren, *Agape and Eros*, pp. 250 ff.; 335-348. Further examination might raise the question, for example, whether it is right to say that "in Tertullian *Nomos* has taken concrete form as nowhere else in the history of Christianity," p. 348.

[5]Adolf Harnack, *Die Mission und Ausbreitung des Christentums in den ersten drei Jahrhunderten* (2nd ed.; Leipzig, 1906), I, 1-16; Kenneth Scott Latourette, *A History of the Expansion of Christianity* (7 vols.; New York, 1937 ff.), I, 31-43.

went beyond the truth of both to the truth which he had found in Christ.

Thereby he did not wish to deny that they had found some truth, as have some more extreme theologians since. In fact, precisely the truth they had found was the instrument for the judgment upon them. Against the noble race of the Greeks, the masters of those who know, the wrath of God was revealed from heaven. In their unrighteousness they held back the truth, prevented it from taking hold of them. God had seen fit to show them what was knowable of Him, in ways known but to Him, and they gained insights into being and truth for which we are still in their debt. Exchanging this truth of God for a lie, they worshiped and served the creature rather than the Creator, who is blessed forevermore!

Except perhaps in the problematic report in chapter seventeen of the Book of Acts, Paul was not a Hellenistic apologist, who proceeded through negation or comparison to show the necessity of the divine being from the being of man.[6] He was rather a prophet of God, who announced the coming of wrath from heaven upon all whose truth had become an occasion for pride, whose speculations stole the fire from the altar for philosophical pyrotechnics. They wrested truth from the Creator's hands and melted it down into a golden calf for them and their children to worship. Now the wrath of God had burned the calf with fire and scat-

---

[6]Guenther Bornkamm, "Die Offenbarung des Zornes Gottes," Zeitschrift fuer die neutestamentliche Wissenschaft, XXXIV (1935), 261-262, note 7.

tered it upon the water and made the people drink it.
Wrath came, not because they had acquired too little
of the truth—at this in past times God winked—but because of what they had done with the truth they had.
It would have been better for them to die in ignorance.

The use of Hellenistic terminology and concepts in
the epistles shows this strain of thought quite con-
sistently. With the formula, "Lo, I tell you a mystery,"
known to the seekers after immortality in the esoteric
cults, he announced a metamorphosis of the body as
a gift of the resurrection of Christ. With the term
"conscience," the comforting assurance to the Stoic of
the continuing presence of the divine, Paul designated
that within a man which would accuse him in God's
judgment.[7] Of course he borrowed from the thought-
world of the Greeks, but he took Greek truth and by it
called Greek life and thought and religion fundamentally into question. In truth, even in Greek truth, the
Christ could not be found. The Christ was to be found
in Him who was descended from David according to
the flesh and designated the Son of God in power
according to the Spirit of holiness by His resurrection
from the dead, Jesus Christ our Lord.

Paul announced a similar judgment of wrath upon
the Jews, who stood on the sidelines and applauded
God's judgment upon the Greeks. If the Greeks were
condemned because of what they did with the truth
they had rather than because of a truth they did not
have, how much more terrible would be the fate of

---

[7]"Even the Greek concept of *syneidesis* [Rom.] 2:15 receives an
un-Greek, eschatological function in Paul," *ibid.*, p. 351, note 38.

those whose truth was quantitatively and qualitatively superior to that of the classical peoples! Paul could have borrowed the horrendous "therefore" of the prophet Amos: "You only have I known of all the families of the earth: therefore I will punish you for all your iniquities."

Here again, Paul did not try to minimize the truth which the Jews possessed, stewards that they were of the oracles of God. From personal experience he knew how the sense of pride at the possession of the law could take hold of a man. If, as Kierkegaard says, purity of heart is to will one thing, then Saul of Tarsus had the purity and sincerity that declared: *fiat justitia, pereat mundus* (may righteousness prosper, may the world perish)! With a sense of genuine admiration Paul ascribed to the Jews a *morphosis* of knowledge and truth in the law, and *morphosis* here was not merely "form" as contrasted with "substance," but rather "embodiment."[8] The law was the embodiment of knowledge and truth, this was Judaism's tragedy and glory: glory because it made of Israel the people chosen, tragedy because it made of Israel the people rejected. Paul knew from earlier days that the knowledge of the truth was the stuff of which inquisitors were made—to the greater glory of God, no less—and he was heartbroken over his people, who had permitted their truth to obscure Christ. It was not enough to know the truth.

---

[8]Johannes Behm, *s.v.* "morphosis" in Kittel, op. *cit.*, IV, 761-762, who claims to detect a note of irony in this passage. The Revised Standard Version's translation "embodiment" would seem to be more accurate than the older version.

One had, by some Damascus or other, to know Christ, and through Him to learn the truth.

In this ambivalent attitude toward Judaism we have one clue to the thorny problem of Paul's use of the Old Testament.[9] At times he seemed to regard the Old Testament as superseded, for Christ was the goal and end of the law as in Romans 10:4. Then again, he seemed to read the Old Testament as a Christian book, written for our instruction, as in Romans 15:4. This same ambivalence has run throughout the history of Christian thought, especially in the ancient church, where Marcion read the Old Testament literally and rejected it, while Origen read it allegorically and accepted it. Very few read it literally and accepted it. Paul's use of the Old Testament cannot be classified under the usual categories of acceptance or rejection, of literal or allegorical exegesis. It was his Bible, given by God, the only one he knew, but now that God had spoken in Christ, it was not enough to know the Bible. Paul's approach to Judaism was to affirm the correctness of its truth and simultaneously to declare that this truth was not Christ, but only a shadow of future things, while the body was Christ's. Knowledge of the truth was a good thing, and a gift of God, but like Isaac, it had to be sacrificed to the living God, and then received from Him once more. Otherwise the truth became an idol and a false Christ.

There were, then, ample opportunities in the Creco-

---

[9]Oskar Michel, *Paulus und seine Bibel* (Guetersloh, 1929), pp. 173-180, and the following discussion of the effect of Paul's view; cf. also Leonhard Goppelt, *Typos: die typologische Deutung des Alten Testaments im Neuen* (Guetersloh, 1939).

Roman world for anyone who worshiped truth to find it. Greek and Jew alike offered him a vast body of truth to learn, to know, and to adore. In Case's memorable phrase, the sky hung low in the first century,[10] and men could find truth for the asking in the market place of ideas. Through this truth they could gain insights into the nature of ultimate being, and in the truth dwelt all the pleroma of divinity. But Paul the apostle turned away—or, rather, was turned away—from all these opportunities to worship truth as a kind of Christ. He was turned to the Chosen One of God, "to have all the riches of assured understanding and the knowledge of God's mystery, of Christ, in whom are hid all the treasures of wisdom and knowledge" (Colossians 2:2-3). In Him he found wisdom and knowledge. By Him, and by His Spirit, he was guided into all the truth, as the Lord had promised. Thus Paul found the truth in Christ.

Yet the wisdom and knowledge and truth that Paul found in Christ were no mere extension of the wisdom, knowledge, and truth available from other sources, as Vergil led Dante part of the way and the Blessed Virgin led him the rest of the way. The truth available elsewhere, like the righteousness outside of Christ, was a truth of the law—and, Dodd reminds us, where Paul writes law, read "religion." The truth of religion, understood as law, was the result of human striving and searching. From man's point of view, the law was a challenge to ever greater effort, in the hope of achiev-

---

[10]Shirley Jackson Case, *The Origins of Christian Supernaturalism* (Chicago, 1946), p. 1.

ing a righteousness at the end of the rainbow. But at
the end of the rainbow, as Luther put it, was Christ
the Judge and the consuming fire.[11] Though the law
viewed humanly was a challenge, divinely viewed it
was a threat and a judgment; for "through the law
comes knowledge of sin." The righteousness of the law,
then, was that which condemned man. So it was with
the truth of the law. The righteousness of Christ was
not a bonus added to what a man had already earned
in the righteousness of the law. Nor was the truth in
Christ written as God's appendix to a book which man
had authored by the truth of the law and his own
wisdom. Only he who despaired of his own righteousness and of his own truth could find in Christ righteousness and truth and wisdom.

It was a question not merely of more righteousness,
but a new kind of righteousness, not merely an added
quantity of truth, but a new quality. For, as he says in
Romans 3:21,22, "Now the righteousness of God has
been manifested apart from law, although the law
and the prophets bear witness to it, the righteousness
of God through faith in Jesus Christ for all who believe." A truth of God had been manifested apart from
law, though the truth of the law bore witness to it—
the truth of God through faith in Jesus Christ for all
who believed. This was the first and foremost charac-
terestic of the new truth that Paul found. It was a truth
in Christ. As Christ was not the pinnacle of human
achievement, but God's gift to man, so the truth in

---

[11]Julius Koestlin, *Luthers Theologie* (2nd ed.; Stuttgart, 1883),
I, 31.

Christ was an unearned gift from the Father, Lord of
heaven and earth, who had hidden these things from
the wise and understanding and revealed them to
babes; for such was His gracious will.

The righteousness and the truth that were in Christ
came to man through the speaking of God. In Christ,
God spoke His Word of forgiveness to man. It was not
Paul, but one who may have been close to Paul, who
asserted that in Christ the speaking of God—the *memra*
and *dabar* and *logos* of God—had taken fleshly form.
The same fourth Evangelist declared that "the law
was given through Moses; grace and truth came
through Jesus Christ." Certainly the idea was Pauline;
indeed, the concept of Christ as the speaking of God
seems to be one of the most universal in the New
Testament, underlying the collections of His sayings in
the Gospels and echoing through the epistles and the
Apocalypse. A study of such terms as *logos*, *rema*, and
allied words suggests that the "Word" or the "Word
of God" was almost always closely tied to Christ. All
the more significant is this in view of the fact that
the New Testament did not use the Old Testament
formula, "And the Word of the Lord came to . . ." It
did not do so, because the Word of the Lord which had
appeared and come to the prophets had now come in
person in a Son, and there was no further need for
the oracle of Jahweh to appear.[12] Christ was the Word
and the truth of God, in keeping with His prayer:

---

[12]On the meaning of *logos* in relation to *dabar* and
memra, cf. Otto
A. Dilschneider, *Gegenwart Christi (Christus praesens): Grundrisz einer
Dogmatik der Offenbarung* (Guetersloh, 1948), I, 200-207; 248 ff.

"Sanctify them in the truth; thy word is truth." After all of man's striving had discovered only a truth of the law that brought judgment upon him, God had addressed himself reconcilingly to the world in Christ, and by raising Him from the dead had proclaimed the forgiveness of sins to the world.

Truth came in Christ, this was its locus. A second insight that Paul had into the truth in Christ was that it came as faithfulness. Bultmann has devoted much attention to investigating the backgrounds of the term "truth" in the Old Testament, particularly in the Psalms. Often it appeared in conjunction with "mercy," until the two became almost synonyms. Bultmann comes to the conclusion that for the Old Testament, and there-fore also for the New, "truth" generally meant faith-fulness, trustworthiness, or reliability. Applied spe-cifically to God, it meant that God did not lie when He promised mercy.[18] The truth of God was equal to the promise of God, and the truth of God was equal to the pistis of God. Theologians have often been much per-turbed by the fact that Paul appears to have used pistis in several ways, sometimes referring to the faith-fulness of God, sometimes to the faith of man. They have tried, often without success, to find a common basis in the two usages. Even more perplexing has been the fact that he often equated faith with obedience, speaking of "obedience to the faith." They have tried

---

[13]Rudolf Bultmann, "Untersuchungen zum Johannesevangelium," *Zeitschrift fuer die neutestamentliche Wissenschaft*, XXVII (1928), 113-163; and the summary article *s.v.* "aletheia" in Kittel, *op. cit.*, I, 242-251.

to show that this meant an obedience to the moral law that followed faith.

Perhaps Paul's use of the terms was more radical and less complicated than that of the theologians. If the truth of God was His trustworthiness in Christ, then the *pistis* of God was His faithfulness in Christ, and the *pistis* of man was like that of Abraham, who did not "waver concerning the promise of God, but grew strong in his faith as he gave glory to God, fully convinced that God was able to do what he had promised." This was an obedience, as Bultmann says, that demanded the surrender of one's own interpretation of life.[14] It was a radical obedience which despaired of being able to fulfil and which accepted Christ as the chosen way of life to God. Truth, then, was not a given collection of statements that somehow corresponded to an external reality. It was God himself being trustworthy, merciful, faithful. And faith was not the intellectual assent that this collection of statements did indeed correspond to that external reality and was therefore "true." It was the obedient reliance upon the God and Father of our Lord Jesus Christ, believing "in him that raised from the dead Jesus our Lord, who was put to death for our trespasses and raised for our justification." The resurrection was testimony to the faithfulness, the truth of God, "who gives life to the dead and calls into existence the things that do not exist."

Christ was the truth because in His death and resur-

---

[14]Rudolf Bultmann, *Theologie des Neuen Testaments*, I (Tuebingen, 1948), 311.

rection man had received the assurance "in hope against
hope" that God meant His creation seriously, that, in
the words of the Ash Wednesday collect, He "hates
nothing which He has made," because He made us
alive together with Him. Christ was the truth because
God had called us into His fellowship through Christ,
and "He who calls you is faithful." The truth came in
Christ, and it came as the reliability and faithfulness
of God, who gave a son to Sarah and Abraham though
they were "as good as dead," and who was as truthful to all who accepted His truth in faith. The truth
of the law may have been information about God and
His will, the truth of the Greeks may have been data
about His being and attributes. The truth of faith, the
truth in Christ, was access to His grace and a hope
of sharing the glory of God. To "have the truth," then,
was to "have God" as He had come in Christ: faithful,
merciful, truthful.

In a more precise sense, however, one did not "have
truth" any more than he "had God" in Christ. Christ
was the Lord, and the truth in Christ was the truth in
the Lord. "Formerly," Paul wrote to the Galatians,
"when you did not know God, you were in bondage
. . . but now you have come to know God, or rather to
be known by God." The "or rather" was well taken. It
was an acknowledgment that the truth in Christ was
no impersonal "something" to be possessed by the mind
of man, and that the priority in the relation of knowledge between God and man was in God's knowledge of
man, not in man's knowledge of God. Here again, exegetes have sometimes been beguiled by the fact that

the New Testament is written in Greek words and they have interpreted the Greek words exclusively in the light of Greek ideas. The statement, "You have come to know God, or rather to be known by God" had a good and a long ancestry in the usage of the verb "to know" in the Old Testament. It meant what theologians used to call a *nosse cum effectu et affectu* (an effective knowledge and response), God's creative participation and involvement in human life. The Shepherd knew His sheep, and only then could He be known by them. The foundation of the Lord was sure, not because man had learned to know all about God, but because "the Lord knows those who are his."[15]

It seems to have been Paul's view that the relation of lordship over man characterized not only the truth in Christ, but the old truth in Adam and in the law as well. In the passage from Galatians referred to earlier, Paul said: "When you did not know God, you were in bondage to beings that by nature are no gods." Even the old relation of knowledge and truth was one of bondage and subjection to a lord. Life under Adam in the old aeon was no life of freedom, which the Christian had now exchanged for slavery to the Christ. In the aeon of Adam, "death reigned through that one man." Now grace had come, "that, as sin reigned in death, grace might also reign through righteousness to eternal life through Jesus Christ our Lord." Though he had the sense of being free and the illusion of possessing truth,

---

[15]Jaroslav Pelikan, "The Relation of Faith and Knowledge in the Lutheran Confessions," *Concordia Theological Monthly*, XXI (1950), 321-331, is a discussion of biblical and historical formulations of this relation between knowledge of God and knowledge by God.

man under Adam had actually come to possess that which eventually possessed him and which reigned over him.

So it was also with what Paul called "the truth of the gospel." It was a truth that laid claim upon man and possessed him, and thus freed him from the dominion of the old truth in Adam. Those who continued in what God had spoken in Christ were brought into a new relation of discipleship. Then they "knew the truth" and reliability and faithfulness of God, and that truth, that truthful God made them free. The reaction to this saying reported in the fourth Gospel shows man's view of his situation: "We are descendants of Abraham, and have never been in bondage to anyone. How is it that you say, 'You will be made free'?" The truth made free, not in that it emancipated man to do what he pleased by the exercise of his inquiring mind, but in that it put him into relation with the Lord of truth in Christ. Truth came in Christ, then, not as a body of truth to be learned or a set of propositions to be grasped by the human mind, but as a new life of faithful obedi-ence to the faithfulness of Him by whose obedience many will be made righteous, that "those who receive the abundance of grace and the free gift of righteous-ness reign in life through the one man Jesus Christ." Thus, truth came in Christ. Truth came in Christ as the faithfulness of God and as that which took possession of man.

Still another characteristic of the truth in Christ was that it came in Christ as a power to make holy. It was part of the truth of the law that it "was added because of transgressions." It came to increase sin and thus, tentatively, to make unholy, "that what was promised to faith in Jesus Christ might be given to those who believe." Romans 6:22 points out, "Now that you have been set free from sin and have become slaves of God, the return you get is sanctification." This is what Ephesians called the "righteousness and holiness of truth" or, as in some manuscripts, "righteousness and holiness and truth" of the new creation in Christ. No ordinary truth in the sense of information would have the power to do this. The Socratic notion that knowledge of the good implied power to do the good and the Kantian notion that what one ought to do he therefore could do were misrepresentations of the actual state of human affairs.

The supposition that what sinful people lacked was merely the knowledge of what is holy, has produced destructive results in education, in society, and in the church. It has produced the assumption that people must be taught truths about God, and then truths about His moral will. Given these two sets of truths, they would then make a connection between them, by means of gratitude or "the third use of the law" or the fear of punishment, in a life of holiness and dedication. The truth in Christ, according to Paul, did indeed make holy, but not by being made into an object of intellectual knowledge. It made holy by acting as a power in the Holy Spirit. The problem of the exact meaning of the seventh chapter of Romans is certainly a knotty one. Was Paul speaking of his condition as a Jew (most modern exegetes) or of his condition as a Christian (many earlier exegetes)? In either case he was speaking of the fact that a knowledge of the truth about what was holy did not automatically carry with it the power to be holy, that, on the contrary, "the very commandment which promised life proved to be death to me."[16]

The truth came in Christ to make man holy because it brought the Holy Spirit. The relation of the Holy and the True, therefore, was not that the acquisition of enough truth would somehow or other make a holy man out of an unholy man. The Holy and the True were related in that the True, coming in Christ as the faithfulness of God to possess man, made him over into a new image by the gift of the Holy Spirit. Barth summarizes this relation of the Holy and the True in the grace of the Holy Spirit: "Grace is the power of obedience; it is theory and practice, conception and birth; it is the indicative which carries with it a categorical imperative; it is the call, the command, the order, which cannot be disobeyed. Grace has the force of a downright conclusion; it is knowledge which requires no act of will to translate it into action, as though the will were a second factor side by side with knowledge. Grace is knowledge of the will of God, and as such it is the willing of the will of God. Grace is the power of the Resurrection: the knowledge that men are known of God, the consciousness that their existence

[16]Werner G. Kuemmel, *Das Subjekt des 7. Kapitels des Roemerbriefs* (Altenburg, 1929) summarizes the several possibilities; Guenther Bornkamm, *Das Ende des Gesetzes. Paulusstudien* (Munich, 1952), pp. 51-69, examines the problem afresh, with special reference to Bultmann's solution.

is begotten of God."[17] About the problematics of the relation between the Holy and the Good we shall have more to say in later essays. But the truth in Christ called forth what Paul termed "obedience from the heart." It created holiness, "not under the old written code but in the new life of the Spirit."

What has been said about Paul's view of the truth in Christ suggests a further question, and an important one. What was Paul's view of the relation between this truth in Christ and all the other truth in the world, especially the truth of other religions? Was it supplementary to other truth, complementary, antithetical, or wholly other in quality? This has been debated throughout theological history, and in our own time by Karl Barth and Emil Brunner. Each has sought to substantiate his position from the first two chapters of Romans, and there the matter has stood. Historically, it would seem that much light has been shed on the issue, and on the meaning of the first two chapters of Romans, by the eighth chapter of Romans, about which, significantly, neither Barth nor Brunner has said very much in their debate on natural theology. Some of the most penetrating analyses of that problem in the history of theology have derived some of their power from the fact that they rooted their understanding of natural theology in a cosmology which—rightly or wrongly or a little of both—they found adumbrated in the eighth chapter of Romans. But since it has been traditional in modern thought to subordinate the ontological prob-

---

[17]Karl Barth, *The Epistle to the Romans*, trans. by Edwyn C. Hoskyns (Oxford, 1933), p. 207.

lem to the epistemological one, theologians have tended
to give their discussions of natural theology a predominantly epistemological orientation, too.[18]

Yet there is cosmology in Romans eight, and perhaps
some ontology as well. Thus the relation of the truth
manifest in Christ to the truth manifest outside of
Christ would appear to be in the fact that the Christ in
whom the truth had come was nothing less than He by
whom the whole *ktisis* (creation)—the same term used
in Romans 1:20—was redeemed and set free from its
bondage to decay and granted the glorious liberty of the
children of God. If in Him all things held together,
then in a language and framework that defy rational
coherence, Romans eight brought the message that
Christ was the Lord of all the world, the light that enlightens every man coming into the world—however one
takes that ambiguous participle.[19] The first two chapters
of Romans asserted that it was impossible to go through
truth to Christ, through the True to the Holy, because
the truth of the law and the truth of being issued only
in despair and wrath. It was the message of the eighth
chapter, put in words that strained even the plastic
vocabulary of Hellenistic Greek, that given the truth
in Christ and the redemption which He offered, somehow all other truth became meaningful, for He was the
Lord at whose name every knee had to bow.

Not through the True to the Holy, then, but given
the Holy in Christ, there was no True which did not

---

[18]Cf. A. D. Galloway, *The Cosmic Christ* (New York, 1951), pp.
40-56 on Paul and John.
[19]E. C. Hoskyns, *The Fourth Gospel* (London, 1940), I, 141.

acquire, by reflected light at least, a radiance and a glory. Paul was not trying to juggle reason and revelation, or to hold reason in his left hand and revelation in his right hand and not let the left hand know what the right hand was doing. Nor did he carefully assign to reason what it could know, and show how revelation completed the fund of truth. Instead, he announced a Lord whose reign was catholic enough to include all reality and all truth. Later theologians have sought to reduce the poetry of this chapter to a theology of common grace or "the uncovenanted mercies of God" or the kingdoms of power, grace, and glory—or, in many cases, they have simply chosen to ignore it. Whatever one may term it and whatever one may seek to do with it, the plot of the eighth chapter of Romans did contain the makings for an ontology of the second article, asserting as it did that what Christ had assumed was "the likeness of sinful flesh." Human existence in the context of a groaning and travailing creation may be seen in the struggle for survival in the most virginal nature, the stench of death coming from the loveliest rose, the gradual cooling of modern man's universe. However Paul is interpreted, there was something to human life in the midst of such a universe that made the Cross not only necessary but possible.

Viewed in this light, all the truth and beauty that human eyes had seen, however dimly, was good and worthy even of the believer's attention. Even of the believer's attention? Especially! For the believer saw it as man's effort to put the questions to which God had supplied the answer in Christ, as man's attempt to see behind his good the Source of all good, behind his conditionedness the Unconditioned. So in Lystra Paul proclaimed "a living God who made the heaven and the earth and the sea and all that is in them. In past generations he allowed all the nations to walk in their own ways; yet he did not leave himself without witness, for he did good and gave you from heaven rains and fruitful seasons, satisfying your hearts with food and gladness" (Acts 14:15-17). Having known Him in the Cross as the forgiving Father of our Lord Jesus Christ, he could look with sympathy and genuine appreciation upon those who knew Him only from food and gladness, from the falling of the rain and the fruitful seasons—themes that have occurred and recurred in the world religions of fertility and spring. It is perhaps inevitable that any schematization of all this will somehow do violence to Paul's intention. From his career as a missionary it would appear that a schematization would certainly be wrong if it invalidated the Christian missionary enterprise. Yet there is still something else that must be said: "Finally, brethren, whatever is true, whatever is honorable, whatever is just, whatever is pure, whatever is gracious, if there is any excellence, if there is anything worthy of praise, think about these things."

From the discussion in the eighth chapter of Romans another quality of the truth in Paul's thought becomes evident, its setting in worship. One of the happy results of recent New Testament study is the emphasis it has come to lay upon the liturgical elements in the New Testament—in the sayings of Jesus in the Gospels, in the sermons reported in Acts, in the whole drama of the Apocalypse, and also in the Pauline epistles, some of whose most important statements have been illumined by the suggestion that they may have had their original context in a liturgical framework. This insight is important not only for textual and literary analysis, but also for the task of interpreting New Testament theology and the theology of Paul, therefore also Paul's view of the truth.[20]

Propositions have not always been the best form for the articulation of truth. As we shall see in connection with Bach, some of the most profound statements of the Christian faith have been not dogmatic, but liturgical. The dogma of the church at a given period can often be best explicated by reference to its liturgy, as the history of the Eastern churches amply attests. This was true of Paul as well. An analysis of Christology in the epistles must keep in mind not only that some of their most explicit. Christological utterances came in the context of ethical admonitions—a fact with which dogmatic theologians have not always been able to deal—but also that they often came in the form of snatches from the liturgy. This was true of the second chapter of Philippians, whatever may be the source of that almost hymnic period. It was true of parts of Colossians. It was true even and especially of the pastorals, where the mystery of piety could be expressed only in a poem as in I Timothy 3:16. And so it was with

---

[20]Cf. Joachim Jeremias, *Die Abendmahlsworte Jesu* (2nd ed.; Coettingen, 1949) for a fruitful use of this insight in the consideration of a knotty textual and historical problem.

Romans, too. Strange it is that the infinite theological
discussions of election and predestination, of determinism and indeterminism in the eleventh chapter of
Romans have so often forgotten that after the search
for truth, which had taken the apostle through exegesis
and history and speculation, came the climax: "O the
depth of the riches and wisdom and knowledge of
God! How unsearchable are his judgments and how in-
scrutable his ways! 'For who has known the mind of
the Lord, or who has been his counselor?' 'Or who has
given a gift to him that he might be repaid?' For from
him and through him and to him are all things. To him
be glory forever. Amen" (Romans 11:33-36). It was a
significant counterbalance to much high-blown Trinitar-
ian speculation that precisely this hosanna became the
epistle lesson for Trinity Sunday.[21] This was, as another
has put it, "the end of the argument" in worship.

That worship went on in the fellowship of the church,
from whose liturgy Paul quoted. Truth was related to
worship because "the church of the living God" was
"the pillar and bulwark of the truth." The truth in
Christ was not something to be enjoyed in secret, it
had to be held in the church: this was the burden of
I Corinthians. It was also the sense of Paul's declara-
tion to those Romans whose truth might have made
them forget the church: "think with sober judgment,
each according to the measure of faith which God has
assigned him . . . we, though many, are one body in
Christ, and individually members one of another." The
truth in the church was a truth that came in the reci-

---

[21]Karl Barth, *Kirchliche Dogmatik*, I-1 (Munich, 1932), 330-331

procity of fellowship, in the check and balance of that
process which has been termed "hearkening to the voice
of the fathers and brethren."

At the same time, Christian truth was always held in
tension, involving the church and its need for edifica-
tion, involving the transcience of the present age. Paul
combined these two aspects of the tension in the word:
"Why do you pass judgment on your brother? Or you,
why do you despise your brother? For we shall all
stand before the judgment seat of God." This was
another criterion of the truth in Christ. The truth in
Christ was also a judgment upon the pride of possessing
the truth in Christ, whether the pride of the heretical
iconoclast or that of the orthodox inquisitor. Any awareness of truth was false if it did not lead to humility before the Lord who was to judge and before the brother
who shared in the Lord's body. Paul pointed out that
the sense of strength in the possession of the truth could
be a deterrent to the life in Christ and could therefore
make the truth into a lie. "We who are strong," therefore, "ought to bear with the failings of the weak, and
not to please ourselves."

Though some theologians who have penetrated most
thoroughly into the scope and significance of the truth
in Christ have tended to ignore the judgment it voiced
upon them, Paul recognized the danger and warned
the Romans: "Take note of those who create dissensions and difficulties, in opposition to the doctrine which
you have been taught; avoid them." Taught a truth in
Christ that united the faithful in the church because
of the faithfulness of God, men could nevertheless make

it an occasion for dissensions and difficulties, schisms and strivings. For Paul it was a mark of the truth in Christ that it united and held together those who were disparate in gifts, training, and interest, that it was a church-creating truth. There were some whose use of the truth led them to exactly opposite conclusions. They were to be noted and avoided as schismatics: "Is Christ divided?" If not, then His body was not to be divided, especially not by the truth of the doctrine that united. Nor was the truth of the doctrine itself to be divided. The word was *didache,* and it was used in the singular. In fact, the only times the term "doctrine" appeared in the plural in the New Testament were when it referred to the "doctrines of men" as contrasted with the Word of God, or to the "doctrines of demons." The truth of God was not an assortment of "doctrines"; it was an organic unity, as Christ was one.[22]

As our first essay sought to show, an equation of the Holy and the True is inadmissible in the Christian faith because of what it does to the relation between man and God. The life and thought of Kierkegaard provide ample demonstration of this. But it is not enough to reject this equation as the idolatry that it is. There is also a category of truth that belongs peculiarly to the Holy. Almost everything which the searchers for truth have tried to find in an equation of the Holy and the True—and more—is available to those who spurn such an equation and seek instead to find the True only

---

[22]The word di*dache* occurs in the plural only in Heb. 13:9, while *didaskalia* is used in the plural in the following places: Matt. 15:9; Mark 7:7; Col. 2:22; I Tim. 4:1.

after dedicating themselves completely to the Holy. An understanding of the True may be one of those things that will be "yours as well" if we seek the kingdom of the Holy One. By the paradox of the faith, he who identifies the Holy and the True fails to do justice even to the True which he worships, while he who interprets the True in terms of the Holy One from whom it proceeds will lose his life for the Lord's sake and the gospel's—and will therefore find it! This was the message of the theology of Paul.

"Now to him who is able to strengthen you according to my gospel and the preaching of Jesus Christ, according to the revelation of the mystery which was kept secret for long ages but is now disclosed and through the prophetic writings is made known to all nations, according to the command of the eternal God, to bring about obedience to the faith—to the only wise God be glory forevermore through Jesus Christ! Amen" (Romans 16:25-27).

In our discussions of Kierkegaard and Paul we have examined the place of the identification of the Holy and the True in the history of theology. But it is not by any means the only way men have sought to domesticate God or to turn Him into a value. Equally dangerous, and perhaps more frequent in modern times, has been the identification of the Holy and the Good. This is the danger confronting anyone who devotes himself to the implications of the Christian faith for the problems of life rather than of thought. A theologian is likely to identify the Holy and the True and thus to become guilty of intellectualism. Most Christians, whether clerical or lay, are more likely to identify the Holy and the Good and thus become guilty of moralism.

Like the identification of the Holy and the True, the heresy of moralism can claim a long and distinguished line of supporters in the history of the church. It has made its presence particularly evident in the thought and work of those men who have come out of the life of the organized church to protest its ethical indifference and to call it to repentance. Whenever institutional

Christianity has come to terms with the world and sur-
rendered the Christian life to the soft comfort of an
armistice with the devil, the world, and the flesh, sensitive spirits have been moved to a proclamation of the
judgment of God upon the sins of church and world
and to a prophetic denunciation of the moral laxity that
had replaced the Christian zeal for good works. In
such a prophetic denunciation, the church's reformers
have often tended to make zeal for good works and the
works themselves the distinguishing mark of the Christian and the indispensable condition of faith, thus
identifying relationship with the Holy and devotion to
the Good.[1]

Because it emerged as such a prophetic movement in
its original attack upon the Church of Rome, the history
of Protestantism has provided many examples of men
and movements that identified the Holy and the Good.
Perhaps the most noteworthy large-scale movement in
that direction was eighteenth-century Pietism in Europe
and its counterpart in England, Wesleyan Methodism.
We have noted earlier that the Protestantism which had
begun in protest against medieval scholasticism eventually adopted its own scholasticism. As the Reformers
of the sixteenth century protested against the baneful
influence of medieval scholasticism upon the level of
moral life in the church, so the Pietists of the eighteenth
century objected to the effect of Protestant scholasti-

---

[1]Thus Adolf Koeberle speaks of Protestant moral concerns that
"have again degenerated into a pedagogical moralism, and seek to
find their justification before God under the cloak of reform, absti-
nence, and vegetarianism." *The Quest for Holiness*, trans. by John C.
Mattes (Minneapolis, 1938), p. 193.

cism upon morals. Pietism and Methodism were both
produced as antidotes to the low spiritual life of the
seventeenth century and to the forces of irreligion
which were advancing with the decline of the orthodox
churches. Over against both orthodox immorality and
unorthodox irreligion, men like Spener and Francke,
Wesley and Whitefield insisted upon a greater measure
of sanctification as the keystone of their program to
bring new life into the church.

While it must be evident to any observer that the
point of view represented by these men did resurrect
an emphasis upon God's will for sanctification which
had been very sadly neglected in the churches out of
which they came, they did not always avoid the danger
of moralism. Especially when the movements they began had gained support and had developed their own
systems of thought, the identification of the Holy and
the Good often came clearly into evidence. Both Pietism
and Methodism have been sources for moralistic theologies, particularly in American Protestantism, and the
type of approach represented by those theologies is by
no means a dead issue even today.

Added to the influence of Methodism and Pietism
upon the moralistic bent of much modern Protestant
thought is the fact that in the nineteenth century there
developed several entire philosophical systems oriented
around the identification of the Holy and the True, and,
consequently, several theologies so constructed as to
conform to these moralistic philosophies. After Immanuel Kant had destroyed the foundations of intellectualism, he substituted for it a moralism as hostile to the

Christian faith as the intellectualism he had repudiated. In his *Critique of Pure Reason* he showed that identifying the Holy and the True was an assumption unwarranted by the structure of the reason, and in this he was correct. In his *Critique of Practical Reason* and in the treatise on *Religion within the Limits of Reason Alone*, he developed an identification of the Holy and the Good and came to define religion as "the recognition of all our duties as divine commands." From this viewpoint it was not a long step to the moralism and "ethical pantheism" of Fichte, who did not stop until he had questioned the objective existence of the external world and of everything else but the moral will, which he then equated with God.[2]

Like most of the philosophies that have been advanced in Western thought, the moralism of Kant and Fichte also had an influence upon Christian theology. The theological movement associated with the name of Albrecht Ritschl represented, among other things, a correlation of Christian thought and Kantian moralism. As the nexus between these two, Ritschl employed an interpretation of the New Testament concept of the kingdom of God, by which men were thought to perform God's will and to bring His kingdom into existence

---

[2]On Kant's moral theories in relation to Christianity, cf. Heinrich Romundt, *Kirchen and Kirche nach Kants philosophischer Religionslehre* (Gotha, 1903), pp. 95-112; also Ernst Troeltsch's summary statement of Kant's viewpoint: "Jesus and the Bible . . . are the classic illustration and incorporation of the Good despite all the morally indifferent matters that may adhere to the Bible and Jesus' messianism," "Das Historische in Kants Religionsphilosophie," *Kant-Studien*, IX (1904), 77. On Fichte, cf. Joh. von Hofe, *J. G. Fichtes religioese Mystik* (Berne, 1904), esp. pp. 28-34.

when they obeyed the moral law. Though this interpretation eventually helped to restore the Reformation
view of the church as a moral community, such elements in Christian faith as eschatology, the doctrine
of the Holy Spirit, and the sacraments were either
ignored or recast to accommodate them to Ritschl's
theory of the Holy and the Good.[3] Coming as it did
when moral optimism was a keynote of Western society
and culture, Ritschlian moralism appealed to man's
conviction that he could save himself by sanctifying
himself. In America, this theology allied itself with the
social gospel; the kingdom of God became a moralized
form of American democracy, and the task of the ministry the proclamation of the "democratic faith."[4]

This brief look at some of the chief systems of ideas
in which the identification of the Holy and the Good
was an important element suggests that there must be
something about it that has attracted men to it. Like
the identification of the Holy and the True which we
have discussed in our first two essays, moralism has
addressed itself to certain situations and inclinations
from which it has derived the loyalty it has had and
still has among many philosophers and theologians.

As we have seen, the identification of the Holy and
the Good has often arisen in protest against a dead

[3]Richard Wegener, A. *Ritschls* Idee *des* Reiches *Gottes* (Leipzig,
1897) is an old and rather strongly polemical study, but it is still
useful; a careful study of the foci in Ritschl's concept of the kingdom
is G. Hoek, *Die elliptische Theologie A'brecht Ritschls* (Uppsala,
1942). See also p. 102 below.
[4]Cf. W. A. Visser 't Hooft, *The Background of the Social Gospel
in America* (Haarlem, 1938); Ernest Thompson, *Changing Emphases
in American Preaching* (Philadelphia, 1943), esp. pp. 212-215.

orthodoxy. So it was with Wesley, so with Continental Pietism. When it has done so, it has sought to recapture the vigor of the Christian ethic in opposition to an ecclesiastical Christianity that had neglected that ethic. One does not have to be a Hegelian to note that the thesis of dead orthodoxy has tended to produce the antithesis of Pietism and moralism. Whenever a church has insisted exclusively upon conformity to its dogmatic formulations at the expense of the Christian life, there have always been prophets who found such insistence contrary to the explicit demands of Christianity for purity of life as well as purity of doctrine. Such prophets have frequently seen that an intellectualistic interpretation of the faith was a device by which to ward off the moral imperatives of the faith. It would seem that this very tendency was sufficiently widespread in the apostolic church to warrant the composition of the Epistle of James, which ridiculed intellectualism by pointing out that the devils were also capable of an intellectual apprehension of Christian doctrine, and which spoke out against any interpretation of justification by faith that would short-circuit the ethical implications of justification.[5]

Thus it would seem that moralism's protest against the excesses of intellectualism not only is understandable, but represents a legitimate and highly Christian concern for sanctification. Several contemporary theologians have recently pointed out once more that God

---

[5]The arguments of Arnold Meyer, *Das Raetsel des Jacobusbriefes* (Giessen, 1930), pp. 113-167, would suggest this, whatever one may think of his conclusions on literary issues.

has given the church not only the gospel, but also His holy law, and that He has commanded the church to preach both gospel and law.[6] Whenever the church has forgotten that it must also preach the law, it has become necessary for someone to reiterate the importance of the law. Unfortunately, intellectualism has often been rejected in favor of moralism, and an exclusive emphasis upon intellectual apprehension has given way to an equally exclusive emphasis upon ethical purity. In view of the stubborn recurrence of intellectualism, however, the protest as such has never been without its merits.

The identification of the Holy and the Good seems, then, to have been a response to intellectualism in the teaching of the church. Another factor that has frequently contributed to the development of that identification is the prevalence of a low moral level in the world around and within the church. In times of moral decadence, Christian thought has often been tempted to stress the moral implications of the gospel at the cost of the gospel itself. German Pietism was brought on not merely by the deadness of orthodoxy, but also by the fact that the Thirty Years' War had succeeded in weakening the moral stamina of the German people. Methodism arose in opposition to Anglican formalism, but equally important in an explanation of its origins is the state of English morals in the days of John Wesley.[7] These two factors, orthodoxy and moral decline,

---

[6]Gustav Aulen, *Church, Law and Society* (New York, 1948).

[7]Cf. Karl Holl, "Die Bedeutung der grossen Kriege fuer das religioese und kirchliche Leben des deutschen Protestantismus," *Gesammelte Aufsaetze zur Kirchengeschichte*, III, *Der Westen* (Tuebingen, 1928), 302-347, on the backgrounds of Pietism in the secular situation.

have combined when the church was so taken up with the development of dogmatic systems that it paid little attention to ethics.

In the face of such a situation, the temptation to equate Christianity and morality has been very strong. The impression was easily gained that the church could afford to neglect the kerygma for a while in order to concentrate on "sanctification," or that the church's chief or only task in response to moral decadence was to draw the ethical conclusions from the faith which its people already, albeit intellectually, accepted. As the Old Testament prophets repeatedly emphasized and as Paul discovered personally and underlined in the introductory chapters of Romans, this has been the lure of moralism. A people which had received the revelation of God's will for man could be deceived into believing that this endowed them with a superior position over other and lesser breeds without the law, when in reality that revelation constituted a judgment upon them.[8] The presence of moral decadence in those "lesser breeds" has only served to deepen the pride of moralism.

Christians have never been the only ones to deplore moral decadence. The rational pagan, too, has found moral degradation disgusting. When such a rational pagan has been a leader of society, he has endeavored to employ all the forces of society to stem the tide of moral collapse. The church is probably the one social force that has been called upon more than any other to perform this task. It is for its contribution to the maintenance of public morality that the church has been

---

[8]See pp. 34-35 above.

accorded certain privileges in society. Society has valued
Christianity for its moral teachings rather than for its
faith, regarding that faith as something indifferent or
downright annoying. Most of the complimentary things
that leaders of states have had to say about Christianity
applied to its ethic rather than to its faith. From the
point of view of the state, to be sure, this has been perfectly proper, for the state has been charged with the
duty of measuring all phenomena within and without
by their possible effect upon the stability of the social
order.

When the church has adopted the same criterion and
has preferred its moral preachments to its religious
testimony, it has fallen into moralism. This has happened easily when the church has tried to relate itself
constructively to the problems of society. At times of
severe national or international crisis the church has
sometimes been led to believe that the only contribution it could make was to bring its moral pressure to bear
upon all who would hear.[9] Such a development was
tragic because it involved a surrender of the core and
center of the Christian faith in favor of moralism, an
identification of the Holy and the Good.

It was tragic for another reason as well, it failed to
accomplish what it set out to do. Society was not in-

---

[9] This is the point of Stringfellow Barr's warning: "I suspect we
could still rebuild the civilization we have now all but destroyed if we
could find the right questions to ask ourselves. But that is not why we
ought to ask them. Civilization would be one of the things added unto
us if we sought first the Kingdom of God." "The Duty of a Christian
in the Modern World" in William Scarlett (ed.), *Toward a Better
World* (Philadelphia, 1946), p. 183.

:erested in distinctively Christian morality. Christian
morality has been far too revolutionary and unpredict-
ible to give security to social leaders, and in some sense
:hey have been more realistic when, like the Caesars,
:hey have aimed to eradicate a way of life that threat-
:ned the very bases of their claim to absolute power.
What social leaders have wanted the church to teach
ind inculcate as morality have been the mores of the
particular society in which the church was living. As
ong as the church equated morality with conformity
:o such mores, it was making its contribution to the
iocial order. Thus, in the nineteenth century, the church
was asked to preach about the sacredness of private
property, and thus to support the institution of slavery.
When it did this, it was praised as the light of the
world. When some preachers announced that in the
iight of God there was no such thing as autonomous
private property and that slavery stood under His judgment, they were accused of seditious conduct.[10] By
:aking upon itself as its primary task the inculcation of
noral principles and by equating these moral principles with the conventions of its society, Christianity has
obscured its distinctive ethic in favor of a sanctification
of secular standards of morality and respectability.

The responsibility of finding the implications of
Christian faith for the problems of conduct and of
:arrying out these implications in the workaday world
ias usually fallen upon the men charged with the direc-
ion of Christian congregations, upon the parish priests.

---

[10]William S. Jenkins, *Pro-Slavery Thought in the Old South* (Chapel
Hill, 1935), esp. pp. 3-47 and 200-241; see also pp. 114-115 below.

Whatever may have been its program or its theology, the church has stood or fallen in direct proportion to how faithfully the parochial priest has sought to implement the faith of the church in the community which he served. No communion which ignores this fact will long endure, and no theology which does not have relevance to this task is worthy of more than intellectual or academic consideration.

Because theology has frequently ignored the central issue of its relevance, the practical ministry has sometimes tended to despise theology, or at best to regard it as a necessary propadeutic device for the cultivation of practical, that is, ethical Christianity. Traditionally, the parish priest has had a healthy contempt for theological hairsplitting and a wholesome concern for the translation of abstract theological principles into the concrete situations that confronted him in the life of the parish. Wholesome and necessary as this concern may have been, it has often led him to circumvent important issues raised by theological investigation in favor of immediate and tangible ethical results, and thus has caused him to identify life in the Holy with a particular form of the morally Good. Such moralism has been a temptation besetting the practical parish priest as soon as he manifested, as he had to manifest an interest in the meaning of Christianity for everyday life. Moralism has been particularly evident in the religious life of American Protestantism, partly because of its historical origins in European sectarianism and partly because American churches have traditionally avoided the abstract in favor of the concrete, the theo

retical in favor of the practical, the conceptual in favor of the ethical.

It may seem contradictory to point out that the identification of the Holy and the Good which has frequently appeared in the thought of an unphilosophical parish priesthood, like the identification of the Holy and the True, can be traced to Greek thought. Socrates was deeply interested in problems of thought and knowledge because he believed that knowledge produced virtue. Aristotle was the master of those who know, but he used metaphysics to undergird ethics. Stoicism evolved an intricate pantheistic cosmology and a doctrine of man, and thereby it substantiated its moral preachments. Creek moralism was not anti-intellectual, else it would not have been Creek. But it maintained that the purpose of knowledge was the improvement of morality. When applied to Christian thought, this viewpoint has held that Christian knowledge was important because and insofar as it led to the cultivation of an ethical Christian life. A theology like Melanchthon's is sufficient evidence for the contention that intellectualism and moralism could be combined into one system, and that the source of both, as of the combination, was Creek.[11]

For these and other reasons, the identification of the Holy and the Good has been so important in the history of philosophy and theology. How completely it has worked itself into thought and even language is clear from the fact that the word "holy" has been modified

[11]Jaroslav Pelikan, *From Luther to Kierkegaard* (Saint Louis, 1950), Ch. II.

by usage in various languages until it is frequently taken as a synonym for "morally good." Perhaps no one has more penetratingly analyzed the distinctiveness of the Holy as an a priori category in independence from the notion of the Good than Rudolf Otto.[12] Such phrases as "holier than thou," such terms as "sanctification," such names as "holiness sect" are all testimony to the difficulty of separating what Otto finally called the Numinous from the concept of moral goodness.

The thinker whom we shall consider for his opposition to the identification of the Holy and the Good is the Russian novelist, Fyodor Dostoevsky.[13] By background and temperament he was drawn to that identification, but his study of human personality in the light of the Christian doctrine of man made him break with it and portray the experience of the Holy in his novels as a phenomenon quite distinct from moral considerations.

Dostoevsky's religious background was the piety of the Eastern Orthodox Church, of which he remained a member all his life. Eastern Orthodoxy has been capable of nourishing deep ethical concern, as is evident from the much misunderstood Byzantine caesaropapism, which regarded the emperor as a high priest. The institution of the basileus in Byzantium is usually interpreted as a sign of the abject surrender of the church to the political domination of the

---

[12]Rudolf Otto, *The Idea of the Holy*, trans. by John W. Harvey (London, 1946), esp. pp. 52-61.

[13]From the vast literature on Dostoevsky, one of the most useful for the problem at hand is a recent essay by Janko Lavrin, *Dostoevsky. A Study* (New York, 1947).

empire, and frequently it was just that. Yet the
union of the church and the state in a single leader
could also be taken to mean that matters of state were
accorded Christian consideration, and that the Christian ethic was a deciding factor in political questions.
As a lay priest, the Byzantine emperor could interpret his
work as the carrying out of Christian imperatives in
the solution of political problems. More than one basileus did think of his work in this way, and the concept
of the Christian emperor as God's priest became an in-
tegral part of Orthodox religiousness. When Byzantine ways were transplanted to Russian soil through
the Christianization of Russia, the institution of the
emperor-priest was one element of Byzantine thought
that quickly took hold in Russia. During the nineteenth
century, the revival of interest in Orthodoxy among
sections of the Russian intelligentsia brought with it
a renewed loyalty to the possible ethical implications
of the Byzantine political theory. This theory could turn
the church into a political institution, and it often did.
It could also turn the state into a religious institution,
and in the thought if not in the politics of some nineteenth-century Russians, this latter was the case.[14]

The impetus which Dostoevsky thus received toward
a moral or even moralistic interpretation of Christianity
was intensified by his own personal background. His
father was a coarse individual, who seems neither to

---

[14]On the origins of this Byzantine conception, cf. Hendrik Berkhof,
Kirche und Kaiser, trans. by Gottfried W. Locher (Zurich, 1947; on
its religious and artistic significance, cf. Clanville Downey, "The Pil-
grim's Progress of the Byzantine Emperor, " *Church History*, IX
(1940), 207-217.

have understood nor appreciated Fyodor's literary and ethical sensitivities. His mother, on the other hand, encouraged him in them. As a result, he learned to hate his father and, as he himself confessed, to wish for his father's death. When a group of peasants successfully conspired to murder the elder Dostoevsky, the son was stricken with the belief that he was responsible for his father's death because he had wished for it. This belief eventually found its way into his *Brothers Karamazov,* in the story of the death of the elder Karamazov and of Ivan's responsibility for his father's death though he really had nothing to do with the actual murder. The shock of his father's murder brought on Dostoevsky's first epileptic seizure, but the murder was merely the climax of an entire relationship between father and son that helped to mould the author's mind in the direction of an advanced moral consciousness.

In analyzing the lure of moralism we saw that the identification of the Holy and the Good has become especially attractive in the face of moral degradation, and that this attraction has been deepened when the church has failed to emphasize the need for a moral life among its adherents. The immoral life of Dostoevsky's father aroused the son's ethical sense. The fact that a considerable section of the Russian church during the nineteenth century had stressed formal adherence to tradition until it was ethically helpless, stirred this ethical sense to action and rebellion.

Historians of the Russian Revolution have often evaluated conditions within the church in the century preceding the Revolution. The appearance of a Rasputin and the influence he managed to wield upon the highest officials of both church and state has been taken as proof of how the leaders of the church had neglected to urge the necessity of Christian morals among the leaders of Russian society. In order to stay in the good graces of the public officials from whom it derived its means of support, the church is said to have muffled its testimony against the sins and injustices of the czarist regime. While it preached to the peasants their duty to obey and passively to accept the ukase of the czar as God's command, it was not as zealous in preaching to the czar and his lieutenants their sacred duty of providing for the welfare of the Russian people. Through its reorganization by Peter the Great, the church had become a department of state, functioning as a clerical police force to see to it that the will of the state was carried out.[15]

This circumstance called forth two types of response from the Russian intelligentsia. Those who were interested in political reform and did not accept the Christian faith any longer turned against the church, adopting the nihilism that Ivan Turgenev unforgettably portrayed in *Fathers and Sons.* Some of the disciples of Marxism at the end of the nineteenth and the beginning of the twentieth century attached themselves to this nihilism. Another group in the Russian intelligentsia, however, was not willing to surrender its loyalty to historic Orthodoxy, although it was equally vociferous in criticizing the empirical church. It was this latter

---

[15]Robert Pierce Casey, *Religion in Russia* (New York, 1946), pp. 1-61, is a more balanced presentation than most.

group that helped to shape Dostoevsky. Hoping to effect political reforms and yet keep their faith, these men demanded that Orthodoxy recover its ethical sense and apply it to the degraded moral conditions in both church and state.[16]

Thus there was much in Dostoevsky's background and temperament that would have inclined him to identify the Holy and the Good. Most of the conditions that have brought on such an identification in other thinkers were present in him. But his study of the impact of the Holy upon human life, as this is reflected in his novels, made it impossible for him to adopt the identification of the Holy and the Good.

The central discovery which made this impossible for Dostoevsky was his realization that sin was not primarily a moral, but a religious fact. Sin did not consist in the mere violation of a law or transgression of a commandment. It was not only that I had done something evil or had neglected to do something good. In fact, it was not primarily something that I did at all, but something that I was. A sense of sin was more than a feeling of guilt, it was the feeling of profaneness and unworthiness. Forgiveness of sin, therefore, was not the act of God by which He forgot a given number of deeds against the Ten Commandments, but the act

---

[16]"Nihilism grew up on the spiritual soil of Orthodoxy, it could only appear in a soul which was cast in an Orthodox mold. It is Orthodox asceticism turned inside out, an asceticism without grace." N. A. Berdyaev, *The Origins of Russian Communism* (New York, 1937), p. 45; on the latter group, cf. Berdyaev's *The Russian Idea* (New York, 1948), pp. 34-71.

of God by which I was made worthy of His fellowship. The root of moralism has been the assumption
that the sense of sin was moral rather than religious in
its derivation, and that therefore the religious sense of
profaneness was based upon the moral sense of transgression. Such a definition of sin has been the obverse
side of the identification of the Holy and the Good.
Dostoevsky rejected it because sin was a religious fact.

Rodion Raskolnikov, the central figure in Dostoevsky's *Crime and Punishment,* is a good illustration of
what the author regarded as the nature of sin. Raskolnikov was a poor student who was having a difficult time
paying for his education. In the neighborhood there
lived an old woman who made her living as a pawnbroker. Coming to the conclusion that as a university
graduate he would make more of a contribution to the
good of society than this parasite, Raskolnikov entered
her apartment, stole what she had there, and when
she came upon him, murdered her and her companion.

Rarely has the psychology of the criminal received
such penetrating analysis as in *Crime and Punishment.*
During the investigation of the murder, Raskolnikov
deliberately cultivated the acquaintance of the investi-
gators and toyed with himself and them by all but
revealing that he was the culprit, then smiling within
himself at his cleverness in evading suspicion. He
wanted to conceal his action for fear of punishment
and yet had to brag about it to someone, for a crime
enjoyed in secret lacked the thrill of a crime that could
arouse the admiration or the dread of others. The con-

versations between Raskolnikov and the detectives superbly delineated this conflict.[17]

Even more significant was the manner in which Dostoevsky discussed the motivation underlying the original murder. Progressively through the entire novel he developed that discussion and in the course of it made clear the deepest meaning of Raskolnikov's sin. The murder of the old pawnbroker was a sin, but not merely because it was a breach of conventional morality. This made it a crime, not a sin. Raskolnikov's sin was brought on by his egocentricity, his assumption that his position in the universe was so important that he could suspend the existence of another person to advance his own ends. He regarded himself as a member of that superior group of individuals symbolized by Napoleon, for whom the universe existed and who could therefore act as they pleased.

Sin, therefore, was not the violation of some precept or prohibition, it was the assumption: I am God. When he murdered the old pawnbroker, Raskolnikov was not responding to an animal urge for blood, but to the human urge: to become more than my limited existence says I am. For this sin he stood accused not only before society, but before God, whose authority he had usurped. Usurping God's power and privilege was sin. A realization that I the creature had tried to act as though I were the Creator produced the sense of profaneness in the eyes of God. And Raskolnikov stooped

---

[17]See especially the conversations of Raskolnikov with Porfiry Petrovitch, *Crime and Punishment*, Part Four, Ch. V (*Modern Library Edition*), pp. 325-343.

to kiss the sacred earth, which he had defiled by his
sin.[18] One would wish that sin were merely the violation of a moral code, for a moral code could be manipulated and rationalized. But if sin was, as Raskolnikov
discovered, rebellion against God, then there could be
no rationalization but only a Kyrie.

In sharp contrast to the pride of Raskolnikov stood
the meekness of another character in the same novel,
Sonia, one of Dostoevsky's most tragic and most beautiful pictures. She lived with her father and stepmother
in great privation as a result of her father's dissipa-
tions. The suffering which this brought on could not be
alleviated unless the family sold some of its property
to buy food for the hungry children. But the only thing
in the family that anyone would buy was Sonia's body,
so she became a prostitute. It was not out of lust or
avarice that she adopted this way of life, nor was she
unmindful of the fact that she was guilty of immoral
conduct. The tragic choice lay between starvation for
her stepmother and the children, and prostitution for
herself. Out of love for the family, she sold her body
into prostitution.

For this she became a social outcast, since prostitution
was a violation of one of the basic conventions of
society. From a moralistic viewpoint she would be
regarded as having forsaken forever the path that leads

---

[18]Sonia tells him: "Bow down, first kiss the earth which you have
defiled and then bow down to all the world and say to all men
aloud, 'I am a murderer!' Then God will send you life again." Ibid.,
Part Five, Ch. IV, p. 407. Raskolnikov kisses the earth: Part Six,
Ch. VIII, p. 509.

to salvation, for she had knowingly and deliberately [1]
sinned against a divine commandment. If the Holy is
identified with the morally Good, Sonia certainly broke
her ties with the Holy when she began to live a life
of sin. Yet in Dostoevsky's novel, this prostitute was a
heroine, yes, a kind of saint. Raskolnikov knelt before
her in recognition of the fact that she represented the
suffering of all humanity. Sonia was a holy person, in
spite of the fact—or perhaps because of the fact—that
she was an immoral person.

Both Raskolnikov and Sonia were guilty of acts that
society condemned. Murder and adultery are the two
crimes that always attract most notoriety and are most
easily judged. Yet there was a vast difference between
the two. In a sense, the immorality of Sonia was beautiful. In a sense, it was tragic. Her adultery was holier
than the virginity of many. The central meaning of
"holy" is dedication, being set aside for the service of
God. Though Sonia broke a basic law of both God and
man, she did it as an act of love—*agape*, not *eros*. Raskolnikov recognized the difference between them and
respected it. He had acted out of an egocentric belief
that he had a claim upon another person's life, she had
acted out of the belief that her stepmother and the
children had a claim upon her life. This contrast, which,
to be sure, bears marks of the novelist's exaggeration,
depicted the true nature of sin in contradiction to mere
immorality. A moralist would be offended at Dostoevsky's treatment of Sonia—she had done wrong, and
wrong is wrong regardless of circumstances or motives.
But in his analysis he set forth the profoundly Christian

and biblical idea that sin is pride, the refusal to let God be God in the truest and fullest sense.[19]

We gain additional insight into Dostoevsky's interpretation of sin from the most famous passage in his novels, the story of the Grand Inquisitor. If Sonia was representative of the publicans and harlots with whom Jesus consorted though they were social outcasts, the Grand Inquisitor represented the proud and respectable, for whom Jesus had nothing but scorn.

Into the city of Seville, during the heyday of the Inquisition, came the figure of the Christ. Like the children of Jerusalem on Palm Sunday, the people of Seville recognized Him and hailed Him as their King. Quietly and meekly He moved among the people, doing good as He had done so many centuries before. His holy pity moved Him to raise a girl from the dead and to restore her to her weeping parents. At just that moment the Cardinal of Seville, the Grand Inquisitor, passed by. Seeing the miracle, he ordered Christ to be locked up. So completely did he dominate the populace that his order was carried out and Christ was cast into prison. There in the prison cell the two met, Christ and the Inquisitor. The Inquisitor upbraided the Lord for having liberated men to a dreadful freedom, when what they wanted was domination. It had taken the church long centuries to undo the damage wrought by this liberation. And now, just when order had been

---

[19]Sonia is "the eternal victim so long as the world lasts" (Part One, Ch. IV, p. 45). "You with all your virtues are not worth the little finger of that unfortunate girl at whom you throw stones" (Part Four, Ch. II, pp. 297-298). "I bowed down to all the suffering of humanity" (Part Four, Ch. IV, p. 315).

restored and men had found peace and contentment
in domination by the church, He had to come back and
almost ruin everything. How dare He return? What men
had wanted in His day and still wanted was miracle,
mystery, and authority. They did not want freedom
and they did not deserve it. Christ had been wrong
in His conflict with Satan, and the church had finally
set things right again. In response to all of this, Christ
was silent. Suddenly, the Prisoner approached the Inquisitor and kissed him on his aged bloodless lips. And
the Inquisitor cried out: "Go, and come no more . . .
come not at all, never, never!"[20]

Unlike Raskolnikov and Sonia, the Grand Inquisitor
was a thoroughly moral person, and he was interested
in preserving public morality. This was why he burned
heretics to the greater glory of God, and why he opposed Christ for having set men free to break the law.
Freedom may have been necessary for faith, but it was
not necessary for conformity to the moral law. That
could come by compulsion, and according to the Grand
Inquisitor, it was only through compulsion that the
common people could be made to obey. The story of
the Grand Inquisitor is easily one of the most profound
parables in all literature, and there are many aspects
of the faith that it enlightens. It is a terrible denunciation of moralism, for the Inquisitor was the epitome of
a moralism so intent upon the preservation of the moral
order that it had no room for Christ and had to be rid
of Him before it could impose its moral will upon men.

---

[20]The Brothers Karamazov, Part II, Book V, Ch. V (Modern Library
Edition), pp. 292-314.

'Such an attitude may be termed moral because it was
·concerned with the Good, but it was sin because it permitted its concern for the Good to drive away the Incarnate Holy in Christ. Thus the figures of Sonia and
the Grand Inquisitor highlighted Dostoevsky's discovery
,that sin was not primarily a moral category but a religious one, and that what determined sin was not relationship to a moral code but relationship to the Holy
himself.

The character who narrated the legend of the Grand
Inquisitor, Ivan Karamazov, gave Dostoevsky an opportunity to document another insight into the contrast
between the Holy and the Good. Of all the characters in
the novels, Ivan was most like the author himself, although almost all the novels are in a sense autobio-
graphical.[21] Ivan represented Dostoevsky's own torments
of soul and his haunting madness. He symbolized the
intellectual who doubted the existence of God and the
devil, but eventually faced them both in existential encounter. This is another way of saying that Ivan's atheism was religious.

In the West, the most popular type of atheism has
been a self-satisfied agnosticism that did not believe in
God because it came to regard God as a matter of little
consequence. The atheism of Ivan Karamazov was quite
different. He, too, doubted God's existence, but his
doubt was an existential rebellion against God. Though
he rejected God, he could never quite escape Him.
The figure of Christ haunted him day and night,

---

[21]On Ivan's relation to Dostoevsky and on the Grand Inquisitor, cf.
Lavrin, *op. cit.*, pp. 119-138.

and in his dreams and half-mad hallucinations the devil
appeared to torment him. His very atheism was itself
a vivid experience of the Holy, and this atheist had an
appreciation of the Numinous far more profound than
much conventional moralistic piety.

Wherever Christianity is viewed as a quiet submis-
sion to traditional patterns of conduct and an acceptance
of social convention, there will be no appreciation of the
atheism of Ivan Karamazov. His atheism begins to mean
something when it becomes clear that the Christian
gospel is a religious denunciation of religion—religion
being understood as man's attempt to relate himself
constructively to the Holy.[22] Traditional moralism and
conventional piety have often put the objects of their
search alongside God and have in that sense been guilty
of idolatry. Atheism refuses to believe in the divinity
of any traditional morality, and in this it is correct, more
correct than some of the external Christianity that op-
poses it in the name of Christ. No distinction between
right and wrong will avail me anything when I am
faced by the awesome and fascinating presence of the
Holy. Obedience to law and loyalty to social convention fall harmless to the ground before His glance.

Western theology received one of its first exposures
to this insight of Dostoevsky's with the publication of
Barth's *Romans*. Here Barth spoke out against the
moralism of Kant and Ritschl that had produced him,
and in its place voiced a recovery of New Testament and
Reformation theology in which God appeared once more

---

[22]Cf. Wilhelm Pauck, "Barth's Religious Criticism of Religion," *The
Journal of Religion*, VIII (1928), 453-474.

as the Wholly Other, whom I cannot appease with the bits of morality I manage to develop. He remains the Lord, and before Him I stand condemned. All the false gods of ethical smugness and theological exactitude must be rejected, religion itself must be discarded, before He can come to give His kingdom.

Barth has thus helped to point up Dostoevsky's break with moralism.[23] Dostoevsky's study of human nature made him see a demonic element in man for which moralism could not account. Like few men before him, Dostoevsky learned to know the subtle means which the demonic employs in asserting itself with the hope of achieving divinity. The temptation "You will be like God" can come in the opportunity to violate the moral law, as it did to Raskolnikov. It can also come in the guise of piety and morality, and it is in this latter form that the demonic is most seductive. Then it employs the sanctions of conventional morality for the accomplishment of its demonic ends. The ultimate and most profound critique of the identification of the Holy and the Good comes in the realization that the demonic in man transcends the moral sense and the ethical consciousness. Therefore, relation to the Holy is far more than accepting or living up to a moral code. As a matter of fact, accepting and living up to a code can be and often is the device by which the demonic ego defends its autonomy against the claims which the Holy lays

---

[23]Thus he speaks of "all clear-sighted men from Job to Dostoevsky," *Romans*, p. 238; and of the anti-moralistic way of measuring human worth "employed, for example, both in the book of Genesis [Abraham] and by Dostoevsky," *ibid.*, p. 122.

upon it. The Holy, far from being coextensive with the
Good, is a different dimension from the moral.

By usual standards, the novelist who brought this insight to fruition was not a sane man. The mental balance which the usual interpretation of sanity recom-
mends can best be achieved if the Holy is veiled through
some other value so that its fury is controlled. No one
who has met the Holy face to face in existential encounter can ever be the same again. Like Ivan Karamazov, he will be terrified and haunted by it the rest
of his life. It will come to embitter his days and to fill
his nights with tears. Never again will he be satisfied
with the contentment that is bred by harmony with the
morally Good. Dostoevsky may have been mad, but
for just that reason he saw through the mask of moralism
covering the identification of the Holy and the Good
and recognized it as a mark of Antichrist.

As we have seen, Dostoevsky was disposed by his
training and by his environment to identify the Holy
and the Good, and he would have been happy if he had
only been able to carry out his identification. But his
madness gave him an insight that is often denied more
normal men. God is more than the validation of our
moral consciousness, more than a lawgiver. He is not
seeking merely to improve us morally, He wishes to
win us to himself again. He will not be satisfied by the
sacrifice of a good life or a moral disposition. He
wants the total man and lays His claim upon the
total man. Nothing less will satisfy Him. A refusal to let
Him rule over the total man is sin. No mere violation
of moral law, no refusal to conform to divine command-

ments, but the pride with which we would hold Him off from us and by which we make ourselves profane before Him—this is sin. We sin against the Holy, and not merely against the Good.

Like Kierkegaard's insight into the fallacy of intellectualism, Dostoevsky's destruction of moralism runs contrary to some of our basic dispositions and inclinations. It seems unnatural, abnormal, downright immoral to believe that God is not primarily concerned with making us good, but that He is out to make us holy, to set us apart for His fellowship. This violates fundamental convictions that have a venerable background behind them in the history of philosophy and theology. It seems to the prudent to run the danger of taking away the Christian impulse toward a sanctified life. To the practical, it may seem like an utterly theoretical proposition that could have been developed only by a madman or a theologian!

In delineating the distinctiveness of the Holy as a reality far transcending the morally Good, Dostoevsky succeeded in stating a profoundly Christian judgment. It may be easier to identify the Holy and the Good, it may be more practical, it may even be more rational and normal to do so. But the Christian faith does not pretend to be easy or rational or normal. It claims only to be an account of how the Holy has addressed himself to men decisively in Jesus Christ. This was the insight that Dostoevsky was determined to carry out, even if it should cost him his sanity. In the twilight zone of his insanity he rediscovered some of the most profound implications of the Christian gospel. As a fool

for Christ, he directs those implications at us, too, calling us into that fellowship with God in Christ which
reaches beyond all morality and all ethics, the fellowship he knew in the madness of the Holy.

CHAPTER IV

THE GOODNESS OF GOD

LUTHER

In our second essay, on the theology of Paul the apostle, we sought to show that although one cannot pass through the True to the Holy, it is nevertheless possible and necessary to move from the Holy to the True, which acquires new meaning in such a context. A similar relationship obtains between the Holy and the Good. Though an identification of the Holy and the Good leads to moralism, the Holy does create its own distinctive category of the Good, even as it sets its own particular qualifying mark upon both the True and the Beautiful.

We shall base this discussion of the Holy and the Good upon Luther, principally because of his keen and prophetic insight into the problem, but also because that insight has not always been present in those Protestants whose protestations of loyalty to him have been insistent to the point of being shrill. It is symptomatic of something in Protestant thought that expositions of Luther's theology are too numerous to enumerate, much less to evaluate in one brief essay, while studies of his

ethic are rare and good studies of his ethic even rarer.[1]
One reason for this situation is the fact that the target
for much of Luther's polemical writing was a moralism
of one kind or another, whose identification of the Holy
and the Good aroused his eloquent wrath. We can better understand how Luther explained the nature of the
Good as well as the problem of its relation to the Holy,
if we preface our investigation with an analysis of the
type of moralism he faced in his predecessors and contemporaries. As Paul's view of the truth in Christ stands
out when contrasted with systems that made a Christ
out of truth, so Luther's view of the goodness of God
stands out when contrasted with systems that tended
to make a god out of goodness.

This was, in Luther's eyes, one of the basic heresies
of the medieval systems. A fundamental premise of
classical medieval theology was its interpretation of
the connection between nature and grace. Grace did
not abolish nature, it sustained and perfected it.[2] There
was, therefore, a continuity between what natural capacity achieved and what supernatural grace provided.
This was true of the sphere of knowledge: reason was
able to penetrate into truth up to a point, and at that
point revelation took over. But it was in the moral
sphere that the distinction between nature and grace
as well as the connection between them became most

---

[1]The most recent such study is that of George W. Forell, *Faith
Active in Love* (New York, 1954); the bibliography, pp. 191 ff.,
provides a rather complete list of previous studies on Luther's ethic.

[2]Thomas Aquinas, *Summa Theologica*, I, qu. 1, art. 8, *Basic Writings of Saint Thomas Aquinas*, ed. by Anton C. Pegis (New York,
1944), I, 14.

explicit. Here the claim was put that if a man did as much as lay within him, God would inevitably supply the necessary additional grace. Man was thought of as having been created with a neutral nature (the so-called *pura naturalia*), to which a supernatural gift (the *donum superadditum*) of grace was added. Grace was interpreted as a "somewhatness" *(quidditas)* which made moral obedience possible. Therefore sin, committed by a nature that had lost the gift of grace, was also interpreted in moral terms. The scope and the character of such moral obedience or disobedience were determined by an elaborate casuistry of the good, the less good, the evil, all arranged into a hierarchy of moral prescription and prohibition. For the task of instructing men in the commandments of His will and compelling them to obey those commandments, God had established His church as an institution of salvation, subordination to which—in the religious, moral, and even political life—was necessary for salvation.

Ranged against this heteronomous ecclesiastical moralism in the fifteenth century was another type of moralism, usually associated with the Renaissance. A generation or two ago there was current in much historical writing an interpretation of the Renaissance, especially in Italy, which regarded it as a revival of ancient Roman paganism in religious thought and as a lip-smacking epicureanism in its ethical practices, interested only in the lust of the flesh, the lust of the eyes, and the pride of life. More sober historical scholarship has radically modified this interpretation of the Renaissance and has compelled less sweeping conclusions re-

garding both this so-called paganism and this so-called
epicureanism. This is not to say that such epicureanism
was unheard of in the Renaissance—not even the most
fervent apologist has been able to say that. But in Renaissance thought at its best there was present an awareness of the requirements of the moral law and a devotion to the Good which compel admiration. It was cast
in the form of a protest against those features in the
approach of the church which sought to superimpose
a set of moral standards upon human behavior but often
left the inner disposition unchanged except for a certain inclination.

By way of contrast the Renaissance propounded a
moralism whose center of authority lay not in the
church and its commands, but in man as his perception
and will came into accord with the will of God. It is
no accident that so many humanists like Valla and
Pomponazzi were concerned with the problem of evil
and the question of determinism, and that the question
of natural law was so prominent in the writing and de-
bates of Renaissance thinkers. These are all questions
which must arise when one seeks to shift the locus of
the moral norm from the heteronomously conceived
church to the autonomously conceived individual. The
fact that some Renaissance men ended this shift by root-
ing moral authority in the state shows that they, too,
were in revolt against a churchly morality but did not
trust individual capacity enough to let it find its own
way.[3] In those who carried through this protest to its
logical consequences, there appeared an interpretation

---

[3]On this trend as exemplified by Machiavelli, cf. Gerhard Ritter,
Die Daemonie der Macht (Munich, 1948), esp. pp. 29-52.

of the meaning of the Good according to which man could find the Good, at least partly within himself, and having found it could also discover the power, at least partly within himself, to live up to it.

Because of its setting, the Renaissance tended to see the morally Good embodied in the customs and ideals of the growing middle class and in the new cult of the "gentleman." A favorite and frequent conceit of Renaissance literature is the compilation of moral maxims for the gentleman, the *miles Christi* (the soldier of Christ), the "universal man." In Italy there arose a genre of poetry perhaps best characterized as didactic doggerel, making up in moral earnestness what it lacked in literary polish and aiming at the training of the young in the way of virtue and success. These maxims, rhymed or not, shared with the common sense and proverbial wisdom of every people the implicit assumption that the heart which recognized the correctness of the maxims could also improve itself by keeping them. They were addressed to man as he was able of himself to recognize the Good when it appeared, and as he was capable of performing it without the overt interference of intermediaries celestial or terrestrial. The ideal they held before the reader was that of the polished and cultured gentleman of quality, the patron of the arts, respectable and normal and charitable, the good man who lived the good life.[4] Two or three centuries later, sections of the Enlightenment combined this ideal with the democratic faith to pro-

---

[4]One of the most suggestive presentations of Renaissance thought, to which this summary owes much, is Ernst Cassirer, *Individuum und Kosmos in der Philosophie der Renaissance* (Berlin, 1927).

duce the industrious and prudent entrepreneur, the devoted public servant and self-made man.

Differ though they did in many other ways, the medieval view of the Good and the Renaissance view of
the Good had this in common, that they both inclined
in the direction of moralism. The moralism of the former
was heteronomous, finding moral sanctions in the external authority of the church, while the moralism of
the latter was autonomous, denying the absolute character of external authority. They were both moralistic,
and Luther rejected them both on this ground. In spite
of his own zeal for the Good (of which more later), he
broke with the notion that the Good could determine
itself.

This was the substance of his critique of medieval
moralism, that it sought the Good in the Good rather
than in God. It had made grace a supernatural *quidditas* (a "somewhatness") of moralistically conceived
merit rather than the unmerited favor of God in the forgiveness of sins. Thus it had shifted the emphasis in
the good life from the Creator to the creature and had
substituted the goodness which man could achieve for
the goodness which God alone could give. By the
medieval interpretation of moral goodness, only that
man could depend upon the favor of God whose moral
disposition made him worthy of it. As a favorite meta-
phor had it, only that shield could reflect the light of
the sun which was first polished and made to shine. By
Luther's view of God, however, God loved the sinner
while he was still a sinner and did not regard the level
of moral goodness or badness the sinner had attained.

This was one of the most notable themes of the original Christian kerygma, and it caused Luther to reject a system which was based upon merit and which eventually found a true representation of goodness only in the professional religious who occupied the monastery.[5]

Luther's polemic against what he called "monastic righteousness," which he knew at first hand, also involved the fact that in the medieval church obedience to the will of God had been equated with obedience to the will of the church, as the word of the church had been identified with the Word of God. So far had this equation gone that the demands of the will of God, as announced for example in the Sermon on the Mount, were said to be attainable only in the life of the professional religious, where they appeared as the "evangelical counsels," while the common people of the church were expected only to live up to the church's demands. This type of righteousness was simultaneously too severe and too lenient, imposing the tyrannical will of the priests upon the people and yet excusing them from the performance of the will of God. In this way it laid undue emphasis upon the moral character of righteousness at the expense of its religious character, and at the same time it robbed the people of the means by which their moral improvement could have been accomplished.

The end result of this process was the virtual obliteration of any distinction between the good life and the Christian life. Partly because of the interrelations between the church and the political community, crime

---

[5]Karl Eger, *Die Anschauungen Luthers vom Beruf* (Giessen, 1900), pp. 44-68.

and sin became almost identical, and the priests, who
mediated the forgiveness of sins, were granted "benefit
of clergy," being excused from trial before the civil
authorities and having their own courts. The state pun-
ished men for heresy, and the church excommunicated
them for crimes against the civil law. To be a Christian
thus came to mean more and more to be obedient to
the mores of the community, for the state was there to
serve the church and its rulers and magistrates held
their positions by the grace of God and the permission
of the pope. In this way the demands of civil righteousness were raised and the demands of Christian righteousness were lowered until they almost touched. In Luther's eyes, this situation represented a debasement of
both the community and the church, both the Good and
the Holy. The community lost the right to enforce at
least a minimum standard of ethical conduct through
its own force and law, while the church lost the power
to create saints in the midst of the common life. This
came about by a metamorphosis in which the distinction between the world and the monastery was
even applied inside the church, with most of the faithful, including sometimes the secular clergy, being con-
signed to the secular world. A moralistic, heteronomous
system, which in the final analysis refused to let the
Holy be the Holy or even the Good be the Good: this
was Luther's final protest against the dichotomy of
nature and grace in the medieval church.[6]

No less severe was his repudiation of the autonomous
moralism which he saw represented in certain phases

---

[6]Rudolf Hermann, *Luthers These "Gerecht und Suender zugleich"*
(Guetersloh, 1930), pp. 155-203.

of the Renaissance. In his early years he seemed to be
in league with Renaissance humanism, to the point that
later interpreters of Luther's Reformation have sometimes interpreted it as the religious phase of the Renaissance or as "biblical humanism." The reason for this
apparent alliance was the fact that both the Reformation as represented by Luther and the Renaissance as
represented by Erasmus were opposed to medieval
heteronomy, although for different reasons. In the same
way Jacques Maritain has felt able to link Luther and
Rousseau because they were both critical of what he
regards as the only divine form of historic Christianity—
though from opposite ends of the pole.

As Luther's reformatory thought progressed, however, the antithesis not only between him and Rome,
but also between him and the humanists became more
explicit. During the early 1520's tensions developed
between him and some of his supporters in the human-
ist camp. One source of these tensions was Luther's
intense preoccupation with the sovereignty of God,
even at the cost of the free will of man. As has been
mentioned earlier, this issue had drawn the attention
of many Renaissance thinkers. Though some of them,
like Valla, seemed inclined in the direction of determinism, the leaders of the northern Renaissance, especially Erasmus, were afraid that such a determinism
might destroy the basis of morality by its denial of
man's capacity to make up his own mind and choose
his own way in his pursuit of the morally Good. In his
Concerning Free Will Erasmus appeared as the spokesman for an objection that has not been unknown since,

as he expressed his misgivings over Luther's one-sided
emphasis upon the operation of God and his apprehen-
sions lest this relieve man of his moral responsibility.
Without an acknowledgement of man's moral capacity,
Erasmus felt, there could be no announcement of his
moral responsibility.

Luther's reply to these objections and misgivings
came in his treatise *Concerning the Bondage of the Will*
of 1525. Though Luther was inclined to regard this as
the best of his strictly theological writings, later
Protestants have not been as enthusiastic in the presence of this essay which seemed to see the human as
merely the profane and did not seem to stop short of
a fatalistic and deterministic doctrine of necessity.
From the premises announced in *The Bondage of the
Will* it was not far to the position that God was the
author of evil, or at least that He let it come so that He
might be glorified all the more. Much of it would
appear to be a living substantiation of Whitehead's
bon mot that "the only alternative to metaphysics is
bad metaphysics." Later theologians who have tried
to follow through on the metaphysics of the treatise
have involved themselves in as much difficulty as have
those who rejected it completely.

A partial solution of the problem would seem to lie
in a recognition of *The Bondage of the Will* for what
it claimed to be, namely, a repudiation of the autonomous moralism represented by Erasmus' *philosophia
Christi*. Seen in this light, its fundamental motif would
appear to be a soteriological one, in defense of which
Luther made use of metaphysical speculation, and some

rather unfortunate metaphysical speculation at that. For our purposes here, the treatise is important as one of Luther's most eloquent and exhaustive criticisms of the idea that the only way to stimulate real devotion to the Good in a man was by assuring him of his worthiness of the Holy. It articulated his urgent insistence upon the primacy of the mercy of God, without which no adherence to the Good could avail or even succeed, and his repudiation of moral autonomy in terms as vigorous as those in which he had repudiated moral heteronomy. Neither the moral will of the individual nor the moral preachments of the church had a right to pre-empt that holiness which belonged to God alone and which was His alone to confer, when and where He pleased.[7] For goodness was not God, desirable though it may have been. The Good was not the Holy, and yet it was in the holy God that man was to seek goodness, for He was "the only eternal Good, an eternal fountain spilling over with sheer goodness from which there flows everything that is good or is called good." Luther's concern, then, was not for a goodness deified, but for a goodness made theonomous, a goodness in God. It is with his enunciation of that goodness that this essay is to deal, primarily on the basis of his Larger Catechism.[8]

---

[7]Such was the thesis of an early work by Ferdinand Kattenbusch, *Luthers Lehre vom unfreien Willen und von der Praedestination* (Goettingen, 1875), setting *De servo arbitrio* into the context of Luther's development.

[8]The latest critical edition of the Large Catechism is embodied in *Die Bekenntnisschriften der Evangelisch-Lutherischen Kirche* (2nd ed.; Goettingen, 1952), pp. 545-733.

One of Luther's most significant insights into the
nature of the Good and its relation to the Holy was
his realization that having the right relation to the
Holy was itself an ethical responsibility, not merely a
presupposition for ethical responsibility. In giving voice
to that realization, he stressed in particular the primacy
of faith. "If you believe, you have" was his motto.
Since this was the case, faith was all-important in
determining the course of human life. It was of supreme
significance what kind of god faith chose. An idol, too,
could lay claim upon man's heart and evoke his religious devotion. Whatever kind of god faith found,
that would be its god—God or synthetic god. Men
differed from one another not so much in the fact
that some had faith and others did not, as in the fact
that the faith of some was directed to a dead idol while
the faith of others was directed to the living God and
Father of our Lord Jesus Christ.

It was not enough to have faith or to have a god. As
Luther had discovered during the time that he wrestled
with the hidden God, faith could choose to attach
itself to the wrathful God who hurled commandments
at it only to confound and condemn it. Such a faith in
such a god could only produce sin compounded with
transgression. The only way to attain to the Good was
by the right relation to the right Holy, the Holy who
forgave sins. The despair of self-goodness and the acceptance of God-goodness was an act of faith, by which
one could make God his God and so appropriate the
forgiveness of sins. But faith which appropriated the
forgiveness of sins could not be a *fides otiosa*, a lazy

faith. "This faith is a mighty thing," it was action, doing, the highest of all good works. Some fastidious followers of Luther have attempted to sharpen the distinction between works and faith to the point that they have refused to acknowledge faith as a work. Luther insisted that faith was indeed a work—created by the Holy Spirit, to be sure, as were all other good works, but a work nonetheless.[9]

Faith in the God who forgave sin thus became an ethical duty, since the command to have no other gods before Him was the first and the greatest commandment and since He was the Source of all that was good or was called good. This was not merely the somewhat nugatory idea that from the right kind of faith the right kind of good life would emerge; that would involve a misunderstanding of both. The good life *was* the life of faith and not alone its result. The handy distinction between dogmatics and ethics, first introduced into evangelical theology by George Calixtus but adumbrated by his more orthodox predecessors, represented a fundamental misunderstanding of the function of both in Luther. Dogmatics was ethics, else it was pagan! The theologian described God and His workings because the God he described was the Creator, and creation not only implied but was the right relation of man and God. Later distinctions between the horizontal and the vertical dimensions in Christian faith may perhaps be useful, but they can also obscure this central feature of religious faith as an ethical requirement. Interestingly enough, they may also ob-

---

[9]Wilhelm Pauck, *The Heritage of the Reformation* (Boston, 1950), pp. 15-23.

scure the religious significance of "ethical" actions and
choices, for they give the impression that these may be
relegated to a secondary and consequential sphere,
which one may perhaps foster or neglect as long as
faith is there.

The debate between Holl and Troeltsch on whether
Luther taught an "ethic of the first commandment"
would seem to involve the question of some such interpretation of the relation between faith and life. If by
an "ethic of the first commandment" is meant a type
of religious solipsism that concentrates exclusively upon
the cultivation of inner piety or orthodoxy and assigns
Christian social action to the functionings of natural
law, then Luther did not teach an "ethic of the first
commandment." He was convinced that the Christian
did not stop fearing God when he came into contact
with other men. At the same time, he did not naively
suppose that the teachings of Jesus and the Mosaic
legislation could become the basis of civil law and replace the *Sachsenspiegel*—the Saxon code. Luther's
ethic would properly be designated an "ethic of the
first commandment" if by this term were meant a view
of the good life in which the service of God was the
Alpha and Omega, in which service to man was not
somehow related to the service of God but was spe-
cifically identified with it, since man was interpreted
not as man alone but as man created and redeemed by
God.[10]

---

[10]For an interesting evaluation of the Holl-Troeltsch debate by a
detached observer, cf. Franz Xaver Arnold, *Zur Frage des Natur-
rechts bei Martin Luther* (Munich, 1937), pp. 25 ff.; on this see also
Forell, *op. cit.*, pp. 20-21, note 7.

This was why, like Paul, Luther could speak of faith as obedience. It was obedience to the God who forgave sin, an obedience that accepted the Good from the Source of all Good because it had no Good of its own to offer. Faith was obedience for Luther because he related it to justification by faith and to the goodness of God. He thus gave to the entire concept of obedience a new connotation. After rejecting moralism because it had absorbed holiness into goodness, Luther posited a morality in which goodness was absorbed into holiness and thus raised to a higher power. In his theology, therefore, the Good received a position higher and more honorable than that which the moralists had accorded it. For Luther, the Good became the Holy, not by an idolatrous identification of the two, but by inclusion in the obedience of faith. "You shall have no other gods before me," this was the first and the greatest commandment. Indeed, when viewed as it was by Luther in its fullest and broadest sense, it could become the only commandment. There was no commandment which was not part of that commandment, as there was no Good which was not part of the Holy who was its Source and Creator.

A corollary derived from this ethical responsibility of having no other gods before the God who forgave sin in Christ, was the responsibility of speaking back to Him after He had spoken His Word of forgiveness. As the First Commandment instructed the heart and taught faith, so the Second Commandment went on and directed the mouth and tongue to God. The emphasis upon this was one of the distinctive elements in the ethic of Luther's Reformation, where it came in course to be known as the "confessional principle." Though in later generations this may sometimes have degenerated into a formal traditionalism, its original form was an expression of the insistence that part of the service of the Holy was a response to the Holy in word and witness. Since the ancient church, "to confess" meant to acknowledge one's sins before God and it also meant to bear witness to the mercy of God in a confession of faith or creed. In Luther's thought, these two meanings were closely connected: there was no confession of sins that was not at the same time an acknowledgement of the grace of God, and there was no confession of faith that did not include a recognition by the confessor of his sin and need.

If faith in God as the Source of all Good was the great commandment, then neither of these two meanings of confession could be taken as superficially as was the custom in Luther's day. He spoke out vehemently against a formalization of the confession of sins in the medieval penitential system, in which men took the name of the Lord in vain by refusing to "fear, love, and trust in Him above all things" while they acknowledged their sinfulness before Him. It was an abuse of the penitential system that called forth Luther's ninety-five theses in 1517. The underlying passion animating those theses, apart from their economic and political overtones, was a predominantly ethical one, the fact that by the indulgence traffic men were being persuaded not to take with full moral earnestness the need for confessing their sins before the Holy One.

A similar abuse had crept into the confession of faith, as Luther learned during the Saxon visitations. People were reciting the creeds without an "inward disposition" and without understanding; sometimes they could not recite them at all! Luther was well aware of the fact that there was a fundamental dishonesty involved in the repetition of a confession of faith which one did not understand. It is noteworthy that occasionally—all too occasionally perhaps, to judge from later developments—he expressed his misgivings about the adequacy of the traditional terminology of the creeds. In spite of these occasional misgivings he never questioned the need for confessing the faith in creed and sermon. That was part of the proper use of the name of God and, as such, it was a moral duty. The traditional Augustinian distinction between the first and the second tables of the law left something to be desired right here. The use of the name of God, a duty that fell into the province of the first table, was one of the highest forms of service to one's fellow-men, the content of the second table. Especially in his sermons Luther repeatedly stressed that it was morally imperative for Christian believers to use the name of God in their relations with others, urging his hearers not merely to provide their children with property and wealth, but also to give them the name of God through their witness.[11] Service to God and service to men could thus be combined in the use of the tongue and the lips for confession. For a moralist, the duty of parents would have

---

[11] On the double meaning of "confess" in the church fathers, see Otto Michel, *s. v.* "homologeo" in Kittel, *Woerterbuch*, V, 217-219.

been to make their children good. For Luther, the duty of parents was to use the name of God to make their children holy by seeing to it that the god they had was the God of forgiveness of sins, and thus to make them good in fellowship with the Holy.

Luther was well aware of the fact that this duty of relating the Holy and the Good involved a relationship to the one holy catholic and apostolic church. His opposition to the medieval theory that the church was the legislator of morals has sometimes tended to obscure the prominent position he assigned to the moral functioning of the church in his ethical thinking. The stress upon the church as a moral community which the histories of theology usually associate with the name of Albrecht Ritschl owed a great deal to Luther's picture of the church and of the relation between the individual and the church in the good life. This may help to explain the embarrassment of many European and American theologians during the debate over the social gospel. Though they recognized its moralism as a distortion of the Reformation evangel, they also seemed to sense that Luther's view of the church contained a more vigorous emphasis upon the moral function of the Christian community than did their own. The research on Luther's doctrine of the church which has drawn so much scholarly attention during the past generation has considerably revised the earlier estimate of the relation between ethics and the church in his thought.[12]

---

[12]Otto Monsheimer, *Der Kirchenbegriff und die Sozialethik Luthers in den Streitschriften und Predigten 1537-40* (Frankfurt, 1930); on the Holl-Troeltsch debate in this connection (note 10), see pp. 9-19, 79-82.

For the problem of this relation, too, Luther's sermons are an important source. In his polemic against the Roman Catholic brand of collectivism, he often spoke as though he were advocating an individualism according to which a man did not need anyone else in order to live the good life. From his sermons, as well as from his neglected polemic against some of the individualists of his time, we gain a clearer view of his belief that the discovery as well as the actualization of the Good was corporate in nature. One was not to suppose, he told his hearers, that he could live out the Christian life without the aid and comfort of his fellow-believers. There were heroic moments when he might have to, moments of temptation and strength and faith. When this strength was lacking and this faith flickering, he could be comforted by the knowledge that he was in the company of a vast cloud of witnesses with like problems and a common Lord. He had to do his own believing as he had to do his own dying, but in his believing as in his dying he was never alone. Again, where one was weak another was strong, and thus each had something to contribute to the common good.

This was not because of any innate goodness in the faithful of the church, or because they were better people together than they were separately. It was rather because the church lived by the forgiveness of sins and because the forgiveness of sins was available in the church, in its proclamation and its sacraments: "In this Christendom, God richly and daily forgives all sins to me and to all the faithful." The church was the communion of saints. But Luther refused to interpret the word "saints" in a moralistic sense and thus make the church a collection of the best people, and he refused to interpret it in a purely eschatological sense and thus make the church ethically irrelevant. He interpreted saints as those whom God had forgiven because of Christ and who therefore shared with each other the goodness which that forgiveness conferred. Membership in the church and participation in its life thus became a sacred obligation, by which one increased his own godliness and contributed to others.

Luther's understanding of the ethical nature of the church's life went beyond this in at least one important respect. That was his stress upon the ethical character of worship. We shall have more to say about worship in our discussion of Bach, but it was characteristic of Luther that he established a close relation between worship and ethics. On the one hand, as has already been mentioned, he made of ethical service to the creature a species of religious service to the Creator and thus elevated morals to the realm of worship. His comments on the word of Jesus, "As you did it to one of the least of these my brethren, you did it to me," reflected the existential pathos of this dictum as well as his appreciation of how completely God had identified himself with the life of His creatures in the Incarnation.[13] On the other hand, Luther also stressed the fact that worship was an ethical activity.

Ethics was a form of worship, but the sanctification of the holy day was also a way to sanctify everything else. If all things could be made holy by the Word of

[13]"Grosser Katechismus," *Bekenntnisschriften*, pp 608-609.

God and by prayer, then prayer and the hearing of
the Word in the worship of the church were important
devices for holiness and thus also for goodness. The
medieval doctors had made the mass a sacrifice of pro-
pitiation by which the atonement of Calvary was repeated daily in the unbloody sacrifice on the altar. This
view Luther rejected. Nevertheless, the mass was a
sacrifice, a sacrifice of thanksgiving, an *eucharistia*. So
also was the proclamation of the gospel. What higher
tribute could one pay to God than to proclaim His
goodness in the preaching of the Word, and to sign His
mercy in the blessed sacrament? The church's procla-
mations and celebrations thus became a sacrifice in a
higher sense than the scholastics had ever imagined.
They also became supremely ethical acts by which the
holiness of God was magnified, the holiness of man increased, and the goodness of man recreated.[14] In contradistinction to all views of worship which sentimen-
talized it into a warm feeling of being saved (and often
saved from the church), Luther's practicality insisted
that worship was an action in which Christians prayed
with and for each other to the Holy One from whom all
goodness flowed, and that worship was therefore one of
the kindest and best things one could do for his brethren. In contradistinction to aesthetic views of worship
which placed it into the perfumed atmosphere of the
high and noble strivings of the creative human spirit,
Luther brought worship into the life of the common

---

[14]On the distinction between Luther's view of the Lord's Supper
and the scholastic view of sacrifice, cf. Regin Prenter, *Spiritus Creator*,
tr. by John M. Jensen (Philadelphia, 1953), pp. 134 ff.

man and taught him to praise God in his own name and tongue.

Luther's exposition of the first table was thus a protest not only against any view of man's relation to the Holy that would moralize it, but also against any view of it that would isolate it from the realm of the Good. If God was truly the eternal fountain spilling over with sheer goodness, then no trust in Him, no use of His name, and no worship of Him was legitimate which was not at the same time a harnessing of the power of that goodness for the improvement of the common life. The practice of the presence of God could be moralized into a mere improvement of external behavior, but it could also be demoralized into an amoral religiosity that concerned itself with the flight of the alone to the Alone in the dark night of the soul. By his restoration of ethics to the first table, Luther performed a service fully as meaningful, if not as well understood, as his rejection of moralism. As we have already suggested, the presence of this element in Luther's ethic shows strong traces of its ancestry in the teachings of Jesus and is one in a series of elements illuminating the extent to which his faith involved a recovery of the life and message of the historical Jesus.[15]

Luther was close enough to the life of the people to know that the mere enunciation of the nature of the Holy and of the derivative character of the Good could not be expected to produce ethical results. If the Holy

---

[15]Cf. Erich Seeberg, *Christus. Wirklichkeit und Urbild* (Stuttgart, 1937); and Heinrich Bornkamm, *Luthers Geistige Welt* (2nd ed.; Guetersloh, 1953), pp. 83ff.

was to be incarnate once more in the "little Christs" as they filled out their allotted years, something else had to be added. To the enunciation of the will of God for holy goodness had to be added an analysis of the structure of the world in which that holy goodness was to act. Such an analysis could conceivably be a cynical affirmation of the reality of the presence of evil in that world and a description of the compromises that were necessary if one wanted to be realistic. Or the analysis could issue in a statement of principles, just abstract enough to be irrelevant but pious enough to provide the form of godliness while denying its power. Luther claimed to discern both these tendencies in the ethics of the medieval papacy, whose political manipulations were as cynically realistic as were its pronunciamentos of moral principles hopelessly irrelevant. In preference to either of these courses, Luther sought to analyze the world *sub specie aeternitatis* (in the light of eternity) and thus to bring the power of the Holy to bear upon the actual situations within which the Christian was expected to be holy as his Father in heaven was holy. With what concrete success he managed to do this is a question not easy to answer in the light of the Reformation itself, and church history since makes the question even more difficult. Here we are concerned with his analysis; about the other problem we shall have more to say later.

Chronologically and perhaps logically, the first of the concrete situations in the world within which the holiness of God was to operate was the family and the community of families. Luther viewed membership in

the family as a divine calling to service, and he laid
such great stress upon this that the larger context of
human society sometimes seemed to disappear. He
was impressed by the fact that in the family creation
and society met, and that it was in the home that Christians first confronted the problem of adjusting themselves to others. Frequently he pointed out that love
faced very few problems greater than those which the
family situation posed, and that there were few places
where it was more necessary or more difficult to see
the concrete human situation as a *larva Dei*, a divine
mask through which He worked among men. The life
of the family was a mask of God to both parents and
children. To children, for through their parents God
had created them and in the parents God called for their
reverence and respect. To parents, too, for in their
children they faced a sacred responsibility and a divine
opportunity for service. Luther had only exquisite scorn
for the professional do-gooders of his day, who were
perfectly willing to do something for the good of society
and for the church, but who shunned the duty and responsibility of parenthood, by which they could have
best served both society and the church. He said that
the sight of one child reared for God should put all
monks to shame. Yet many parents were neglecting
this responsibility, so that "One fool trains another, and
as they have lived, so their children live after them."[16]

It was a major function of civil government to order
society and social life in such a way that the family
would be enabled to do this task. This was one reason

---

[16]Werner Elert, *Morphologie*, II, 80-99; Forell, op. *cit.*, pp. 127-129.

for Luther's insistence upon the maintenance of social order as the primary function of government and for his fear of anarchy. It was the calling of most men to be fathers, it was the calling of the prince to see to it that the fathers could carry out their calling. Thus Luther was not primarily concerned with government as an agency by which men expressed and carried out their collective will for the common good in the social order. Such an interpretation of government would have put man at the center and sought the common good either in one man seen as man (this would have been autocracy) or in the entire group of men seen as men (this would have been democracy). Luther was concerned with government of whatever kind as an agency by which God exercised His will for order and peace. The difference between Lutheranism and Calvinism in this regard was not that Calvinism advocated theocracy while Lutheranism did not, but that Calvinist theocracy was actually a "bibliocracy"—to coin a somewhat barbaric expression—in which the Bible ruled the civil estate. Luther wanted to see God rule, but for ruling God had called, as His agents, the princes, not the clergy or the expositors of the Scriptures.

The history of the relation between Lutheranism and government is evidence that this ideal has not always been realized, for whatever reasons. When all the apologists for Luther have finished their recitation of passages in which he stressed the moral nature of government, the fact remains that his ethic of the family was far more completely articulated than his ethic of the

state, and that this has been true for much of Lutheranism since. Such apologies could perhaps be strength-
ened by pointing out that what was important for most
people in Luther's Germany, and perhaps for most
people in most times, was that God should work
through parents and children in such a way that the
home might become a holy temple, while the affairs
of state were of immediate interest to them only to the
extent that they impinged upon the common life.
Luther's defense of the domestic interests of these little
people may have been no less praiseworthy than the
ideals of those revolutionaries who tried to make every
man a king, and a political scientist in addition, whether
or not he had the competence, training, or calling to
rule.[17] Since Luther was interested in the way the holiness of God created the goodness of man, his primary
concern was with the home, where everyone had a
calling for direct service, rather than with the state,
where only some had a direct calling. This factor, inci-
dentally, would make impossible the direct application of Luther's political ethic to the vastly diffused
responsibilities of the modern political community.

Society, especially as represented in the family, was
a creation of God and, as such, one of the most elemental contexts within which the Christian Good was
to operate. Even more elemental a context was life
itself, and on this subject Luther had much to say. Life
itself was a divine creation, and one who wanted to
relate the good life to the Holy had therefore to develop a view of life that was derived from the creative

---

[17]Cf. Ottmar Dittrich, *Luthers Ethik* (Leipzig, 1930), pp. 107-116.

will of God. Later theologians have summarized this viewpoint in the term "order of creation." By its use to justify many good things and many evil things— monogamy, monarchy, slavery, war, laissez-faire capitalism, to name only a few—this term has almost disqualified itself as a semantically useful tool.[18] The correct thing that it wanted to say was that for Luther the fundamental structure of the good life was determined by the creative activity of God and not by the initiative of man. Luther gave voice to this in particular when he took up the sacredness of life.

At just this point a basic difference between Luther and some of his interpreters needs emphasis. For Luther at his best, the basic distinction in theology was not between God as He is and man as he is, the Infinite and the finite, though he certainly maintained such a distinction. The basic distinction was between God as the Holy and man as sinner. He could, therefore, regard life as sacred without in any way violating the holiness of God. The holiness of life was derivative, as life itself was derivative. As a creation, and a creation in the image of God at that, human life was possessed of a certain invested holiness. To kill meant therefore to lay profane hands upon that which, by the creation of the Holy One, was holy and set aside for His purposes. Reverence for God necessarily involved, and did not merely imply, reverence for the life which He had created and which, in Jesus Christ, He had assumed. To kill also meant to forget the first commandment,

---

[18]Elert, *Morphologie*, II, 37-49; Reinhold Niebuhr, *The Nature and Destiny of Man*, II (New York, 1943), 197-198.

"that He is our God, that is, that He will help, assist, and protect us, in order thus to quench the desire for revenge in us."[19]

An allied motif was at work in Luther's ethical evaluation of the universe. Since the Enlightenment, Western men have lived in what Hirsch has recently called "a disenchanted world." Luther most certainly did not. Unenlightened and unencumbered by the results of modern science, he had the happy gift of seeing in the whole cosmos the invested holiness which it had received from its Creator. Therefore the reverence for life which the Fifth Commandment enjoined could be applied to all the life of the universe, sharing as it did in the creation of God and in the curse of sin. Surely a recovery of the sense of the holiness of the earth as God's creation is one of the most pressing needs in the ethical thought of contemporary men, and the fact that it has received more eloquent expression from conservationists and agriculturists like Louis Bromfield than from theologians only accentuates the need. There is a line beyond which man's tampering with the earth, from which he came and to which he must return, is blasphemous. The fact that such a line is very difficult to draw does not relieve us of the responsibility of drawing it, as Justice Holmes once observed. Luther recognized that man's companions in earth shared his creation and therefore his shame and therefore his glory, and he saw reverence for life as a moral imperative contained in the very concept of creation.[20]

[19]Gustaf Wingren, *Gott und Mensch bei Karl Barth* (Berlin, 1951), p. 23, note 58.
[20]Bornkamm, *op. cit.*, pp. 202 ff.

This attitude also helps to explain his ethics of sex. The muckraking research of Father Grisar has uncovered a thesaurus of invective in Luther's writings that would make many a modern Protestant blush. Luther's defenders have feverishly explained, not without some condescension, that he was a "child of his time," which was given to foul language. This undoubtedly explains many of Luther's more earthy expressions, but it would be worth asking whether the term "earthy" in this connection may not have religious meaning as well. One does not have to be a devotee of the literature of the four-letter word—much of which is merely a striving for effect and for profit—to acknowledge that there is present in some of it a yearning for the stolen innocence of Paradise lost and for the elemental view of the body and of human passions as a good gift from the goodness of God. God is not against sex—after all, He created it! Luther described his relations with his wife in terms so naive as to belie his monkish training, and much of his supposed immodesty was a chaste and childlike appreciation of the God who had made and redeemed all of life, not merely the disembodied spirit.

God had therefore "created man and woman separately (as is evident), not for lust, but so that they might live together, be fruitful, beget children, and nourish and train them to the glory of God." This was a nobler and a more chaste work than that of many who resisted God's order and command, despising and forbidding marriage. Against such a false asceticism Luther taught a view of marriage in which evil was removed not by denying the creation, but by giving it its true meaning in the Creator. True chastity was possible in marriage—indeed, except for those few endowed with a supernatural gift, it was possible only in marriage. Luther also directed his view of marriage against a false self-assertiveness, which, he said, was often combined with professional asceticism. Marriage was good and sex was noble not in themselves, but as part of the creative activity of God. The sin was either to spurn them as though one were too good for that which God had created, or to abuse them as though they belonged to man and not to God. By his unique interpretation of the relation between the Holy and the Good in the ethics of sex, Luther could avoid both prudery and profligacy and thus could see in sex both its temptations to sin and its possibilities for divine service.[21]

Luther's attitude toward property had a similar orientation. The alternatives of prudishness and profligacy were represented in this question, on the one hand, by the poverty ideal of the medieval church and the communism of some of the sects, and, on the other hand, by the surging drive for power in the growing bourgeoisie. There was a communist trend throughout the history of the medieval church, becoming articulate in such groups as the spiritual Franciscans and coming into its own with various sectarians of the Reformation.

---

[21]See the references in note 16 above; an examination of the passages blushingly recited in the polemical work of Siegmund Baranowski, *Luthers Lehre von der Ehe* (Muenster, 1913), pp. 49-83, bears out this feature of Luther's sex-ethic, contrary to the author's intentions.

Luther regarded this as a denegation of the goodness of God in the material things of life, and he spoke eloquently of the generosity with which God had provided so many good things for man to possess. But "to possess" actually meant to hold in trust, for, as Luther asserted against the rising spirit of capitalism, autonomous private property was unthinkable if God was truly the Holy One.[22] Property was just another of the settings within which the Christian's attitude of having nothing, yet possessing everything could display itself. Luther often repeated the apostolic word: "All are yours; and you are Christ's; and Christ is God's." Therefore property—like the family, like this body and life, like sex—could be made holy by the Word of God and prayer. With all of life and with the world itself, it could be sacramentalized for him who knew God as the Source of all Good and who knew all Good as the created gift of the Holy.

As has already been mentioned, the history of Protestant ethical thought raises a number of serious problems. The controversy between Amsdorf and Major, issuing in the fourth article of the Formula of Concord, illustrates what difficulty the generation of Lutheran theologians after Luther discovered in trying to foster an evangelical morality without lapsing into moralism. The Pietist and Methodist controversies of the eighteenth century furnish additional evidence of the fact that zeal for the purity of the Word has not always

[22]This issue has been treated in the recent study of Hermann Barge, *Luther und der Fruehkapitalismus*, No. 168 of "Schriften des Vereins fuer Reformationsgeschichte" (Guetersloh, 1951).

been matched by equal zeal for the purity of life. The
theological literature of modern Protestantism in Europe
and in America suggests that this problem is more easily
raised than solved.[23]

On the practical level, the situation may be a little
better, but not much better. The ethical embarrassment
of Protestantism has expressed itself there in a kind of
oscillation between the proclamation of the historical
kerygma with its doctrinal implications, and a dogged
form of moral admonition more or less based upon that
kerygma. This oscillation has proceeded on the hope
that if the hearer is subjected often enough to both kinds
of preaching, the Holy Spirit will undoubtedly lead
him to holiness. Yet the problem remains for every theologian and preacher. Luther's repudiation of moralism
lends itself easily to application in later theological and
political situations, while a repetition of his ethic in
later situations has often proved to be impossible. Similarly, evangelical Protestantism has usually been much
more eloquent in its denunciations of moralism than in
its pronunciation of morality, and its excursions into
ethics have not always been true to its basic theological
convictions.

The basic theological convictions of evangelical Protestantism proceed from Luther's realization that while
the Good and the Holy were not identical, the Good
was available as a gift from the Holy in the forgiveness

---

[23]Cf. the brief notes and comments of Leonhard Fendt, "Die Heili-
gung bei Luther," *Zur Theologie Luthers*, No. 4 of "Schriften der
Luther-Agricola Gesellschaft in Finnland" (Helsinki, 1943), pp. 15
42; also Johann Haar, *Initium Creaturae Dei* (Guetersloh, 1939), pp
82-116.

of sins. For Luther this realization meant a thorough reinterpretation of the Good as it worked itself out in the context of nature and history. Just as the power of the Holy whom Luther confronted in Christ meant the obliteration of all self-made goodness, so in the lives of his followers the grace of the Holy can mean the creation and recreation of the human Good by relating it to the eternal Fountain spilling over with sheer goodness, from which flows everything that is good or is called good, and which has burst into human life in Jesus Christ our Lord, the mirror of the goodness of the fatherly heart of God.

During the course of our discussion thus far we have examined the two most frequent attempts in Western thought to classify the Holy under some value, the identification of the Holy with the True and with the Good. Stated in traditional philosophical categories, this means that the Holy cannot be subsumed under either metaphysics or ethics. A third among the classical divisions of philosophy has also been called upon to absorb the Holy—aesthetics, the doctrine of the Beautiful. In many ways the subtlest and most appealing of the attempts to domesticate the Holy, aestheticism has sought within the fascination which the Beautiful holds for men an explanation of the fascination of the Holy.

Like both intellectualism and moralism, aestheticism gained currency among the Greeks. The earliest Greek minstrels seem to have been regarded by their contemporaries as mouthpieces of the gods. Even though calling upon the muses for aid in the composition of an epic may have degenerated into a mere poetic device in later days, it seems quite clear that at least for the bards whose works were combined into the Homeric

118

corpus this prayer sprang from the genuine religious conviction that the gods employed the beauties of man's poetic creativity to reveal their nature and will to men. Among the earliest productions of Greek artistic genius were statues and busts of the gods. Greek architecture owed much of its origins to the need for temples, and it was believed that the gods themselves inspired architect and artist to create buildings of a type which would be worthy of the divine use for which these buildings were to be set aside.

The highest achievement of the Greek artistic and religious genius was the Greek drama. In its drama rather than in its philosophy the Greek mind came to grips with the deepest and bitterest realities of human existence. It is strange that early Christianity, with its profound sense of tragedy and redemption, should have paid so little attention to Greek tragedy and so much to late Greco-Roman philosophy. Greek tragedy embodied the best that Greece was able to discover about the paradox of human life in its relation to the ultimates under which it is lived. In passages of moving religious content, Sophocles' choruses described the sense of defeat and frustration epitomized by Oedipus as the law of existence: that the very devices by which I would seek to escape my destiny have become tools in its hands for the realization of my inexorable destiny. By thus making its poets rather than its philosophers the stewards of the mysteries, Greek culture set a pattern of close identification between religion and the arts that was to persist in the West long after both the art form

which they used and the religion for which they used it
had become objects of only antiquarian interest.[1]

As Greek philosophy provided the metaphysical
framework within which much of Christian theology
was cast, so the Greek drama was instrumental in the
development of Christian devotional and liturgical
forms. Students of liturgical history have traced the
interrelations of drama and liturgy, indicating that much
medieval drama was derived from liturgy and, similarly, that much medieval liturgy was derived from
drama. That feature is even more pronounced in Eastern worship forms than in the Roman Catholic, partly
because the Eastern church retained the use of the
Greek language and with it a continuity with Greek
culture much more direct than that of the West.

Medieval mysticism was another element that per-
petuated the identification of the Holy and the Beautiful. The mystical cultivation of an intimate and immediate communion with God brought with it a charg-
ing of the emotions in which aestheticism could make a
stirring appeal. Sometimes in opposition to extreme intellectualism and sometimes in company with scholastic
theology, medieval mysticism directed the believer to a
union with God that transcended mere intellectual
knowledge. The visions of St. Hildegard of Bingen or
in the period of the Reformation, of the celebrated St.
Theresa revelled in the contemplation of the beautiful
presence of the indwelling Christ. The strongly sexual
overtones in some of the visions of ascetic women in the

---

[1]On the religious functions of Greek drama, see Werner Jaeger
interpretation of Aeschylus, *Paideia*, I, 266-267.

Middle Ages serve to highlight the confusion of the adoration of Christ with the enjoyment of aesthetic rapture, which, in turn, has affinities with the delicate and deep urgings of sex.[2]

Aestheticism, then, has often appeared when religion was put into an emotional framework, and especially when the emotions were in an advanced state of refinement. One would expect, therefore, that the influence of Kant should sometimes have resulted in an identification of the Holy and the Beautiful. Although Kant removed religion from the intellectual sphere to put it into the moral, as we saw earlier, many of those who followed him preferred to root the religious consciousness in the emotions rather than in the moral will. Among these latter, the German poet Schiller occupied a prominent place. Virtually all of Schiller's philosophical writings were addressed to the problem of aesthetics, on the basis of Kant's philosophy. Schiller accepted Kant's conclusion that the real explanation and meaning of human life could not be gained by intellectual processes alone, but he believed that Kant had sold the aesthetic short in his desire to elevate the moral.

In an effort to repair this inadequacy in Kant, Schiller hoped to effect a synthesis of the Good and the Beautiful. Here he showed his affinity to the Greek tradition. Its highest ideal was *kalokagathia*, originally the mark of the aristocrat but later developed by Plato and Aris-

---

[2]Hermann Bechmann, *Evangelische und katholische Froemmigkeit m Reformationszeitalter, dargestellt an Martin Luther und Teresa di esu* (Munich, 1922); Henry Osborn Taylor, *The Medieval Mind* (4th ed.; London, 1938), I, 458-486.

totle as the characteristic quality of the gentleman. The ideal of *kalokagathia* assumed a relationship between a man's physical beauty and his moral quality, and by encouraging the development of both in harmony with each other it produced the standard of gentlemanly excellence exemplified in men like Pericles. Schiller searched for a similar synthesis on the basis of Kant. He saw in the combination of beauty and goodness a fundamental quality of nature, and he urged the training of aesthetic sensitivity as a means of achieving moral quality and inner harmony.[3]

It was not through Schiller but through his younger contemporary Schleiermacher that the glorification of emotional and aesthetic sensitivity entered into Christian thought. Once more, the classical influence was an impelling force in this direction. Through his study of Plato, Schleiermacher's thinking had been molded by the Greek idea of symmetry and of balance in both art and life. When he defined religion as a feeling of utter dependence, he was protesting against both intellectualism and moralism, the intellectualism of Orthodoxy and the moralism of Kant. As can be seen from his sermons, Schleiermacher addressed his religious appeals to the emotions. His sermons would move his audience to tears, and some of his listeners became hysterical.

---

[3]Schiller's statement of his aesthestic theory in relation to Kant appears in his essay of 1793-1794, "Vom Erhabenen," subtitled "Zur weiteren Ausfuehrung einiger Kantischen Ideen," *Schillers Werke*, V (Berlin, 1927), 184-235. Cf. Israel Knox, *The Aesthetic Theories of Kant, Hegel, and Schopenhauer* (New York, 1936), pp. 69-76; and Eugen Kuehnemann, *Kants und Schillers Begruendung der Aesthetik* (Munich, 1895), esp. pp. 89-99. On the significance of *kalokagathia*, see Jaeger, op. *cit.*, II, 194; and Walter Grundmann, *s. v.* "kalos" in *Kittel, Woerterbuch*, III, 540-542.

Even today, with a full century intervening, the sermons of Schleiermacher have the power to stir. As a good classicist, Schleiermacher grasped the balance of the ancients, emotion controlled by form.

This balance was also the ideal of the German Romantics, though the emotion sometimes overwhelmed the form. They were impressed with the ineffable quality of religious sentiment, and saw a close relationship between that sentiment and the reaction evoked by the observation of the Beautiful in art and literature. For this reason, many of them were seized with a profound nostalgia for what came erroneously to be termed "the age of faith" and for the harmony of the Holy and the Beautiful they saw there. Such a nostalgia for the Middle Ages, which is still evident in many modern aesthetes, led some of the Romantics to embrace a quasi-aesthetic Roman Catholicism, revelling in mystical surrender and serene contemplation of the nobility in God and Gothic. Carried away by the serenity of a Madonna or the sweep of a cathedral, a mind conditioned to demand emotional satisfaction and exhilaration from religion came eventually to identify this Beautiful with the Holy. Whatever else it may mean, much of modern art would appear to be a pessimistic by-form of the same romanticism.[4]

It is understandable that the identification of the Holy and the Beautiful has had such an allure for men since ancient Greece, for it has appealed to some of the highest and noblest stirrings of the human spirit.

---

[4]For a critique of nineteenth-century aestheticism, cf. Werner Elert, *Der Kampf um das Christentum* (Munich, 1921): "Kultur ohne Christentum," pp. 310 ff.

To a greater extent than either intellectualism or moralism, aestheticism has been able to satisfy yearnings deep within the human breast. For that reason, those who had possessed the Beautiful could very easily be deluded into supposing that they had taken hold of the Holy itself.

Such a supposition was only intenstified by the subordination of both the Holy and the Beautiful to either the True or the Good in the history of Western thought. When a protest has arisen against such a subordination, supporters of religion and supporters of art were easily allied with each other and came to believe that they were defending the same or similar values. Intellectualism has tried to domesticate God by subjecting the Holy to truth and knowledge, but it has also attempted to reduce the Beautiful to a set of rules and has claimed to be able to explain away all artistic productions by the use of physics or neurology, spectroanalysis or psychoanalysis. Similarly, moralism has not only categorized the Holy as the validation of the morally Good. When it has dealt with art and literature, it has applied the canons of a preconceived morality to artistic and literary compositions. It has eventually clamped down on any free expression of artistic creativeness and denied the artist's freedom to depict life as he saw it. Instead it has insisted that all art should be didactic, that every novel should teach a moral, and that virtue should always triumph.[5]

---

[5]One of the most familiar defenses of art (and therefore religion!) against this tendency is Ralph Waldo Emerson's essay, "The Poet," *The Complete Essays and Other Writings* (New York, 1940). pp. 320-364, esp. pp. 332 ff.

Now with the discovery that neither intellectualism nor moralism was an adequate description of the impact of the Holy upon human life, and that neither of them had done justice to the basic appeal that the Beautiful could make, the conclusion lay at hand that over against the True and the Good, the Holy and the Beautiful lay in the same general area of life. This may have been the conclusion which Schleiermacher drew in repudiating both intellectualism and moralism in favor of a wistful and aesthetic emotionalism.

The close tie of the Holy and the Beautiful can be seen in more than this negative alliance. As was evidenced by ancient Greek culture, both art and religion have been able to claim the loyalty of the human heart because they professed to reveal a mystery not accessible by any other means. The qualification "What no eye has seen, nor ear heard" could apply to both the Holy and the Beautiful. As the high priest of the mysteries of the Beautiful, the artist or poet could bring a new charm to what had been drab and commonplace. He could put the ordinary affairs of life in a new light, endow the physical world with what could be called a "sacramental" significance, that is, a meaning it did not intrinsically possess but acquired by the "word" spoken to it. No level of knowledge would guarantee an understanding or appreciation of the Beautiful, for it did not reside in the nature of things but was received by a sort of revelation. The function of the artist was to draw the Beautiful out of the physical that men might see and adore it. From this essentially classical interpretation of the nature of art and of the function of the artists, the parallels of art and religion come into focus.

As both art and religion have claimed to make known a mystery, so they have used a similar means to communicate this mystery. Neither has made the claim that it could bring men face to face with the mystery without the aid of a mediator. Rather, both have mediated the mystery to man through the use of symbols calculated to reveal only as much of the mystery as man could or should understand. In the world of art, this revelation has been accomplished by several means. To inculcate an abstract idea or principle, the artist has put it into concrete form, a figure or a color or the character in a drama or a melody. A painter was not expected to be literal and accurate in his reproduction of the subject. On the contrary, a painting was distinguished from a photograph by its judicious selection of details in order to reveal more about the subject than the undiscriminating and candid eye of the camera could. By its very nature, then, the painting was a misrepresentation, and yet the misrepresentation could be a more reliable index to the true nature of the subject than a photograph.

In their myths and sacred histories, the world religions have operated with the same sort of representation. Even the theophanies of the Old Testament gave God a form, human or otherwise, in order to reveal to men an insight into His nature which they could not gain by beholding Him, as Luther said, "In His naked majesty." Religion has always been incurably anthropomorphic. Its descriptions of God have of necessity borrowed analogies from the world of human experience and sense. The Psalms called God, among other things, a father, a shepherd, a man of war, a rock, a fortress, a husband. In reality, of course, He was none of these things, and the prophets readily admitted, in fact they demanded, that no one should take these analogies as more than symbols. Yet symbols they were, to be taken seriously though not literally, for they mediated the true nature of God. The peculiar nature of symbols is that at the same time they conceal and reveal, that they reveal by concealing.[6]

The supreme instance of this is the Incarnation. It was the central affirmation of the Christian kerygma that the Son of the living God had assumed human and historical form in Jesus Christ, and that Christ was therefore the personal revelation of God himself. But the kerygma asserted that Christ was, to use Kierkegaard's apt phrase, God's Incognito. In Him God was revealed, in Him God was concealed: only faith could come to terms with this paradox. What concerns us in our present discussion is the underlying relationship between this Christian view of the embodiment of the Son of God in the person of Jesus Christ and the function of the symbolic in art. Nietzsche summarized that function very well when he termed art a *Mittelwelt*—an intermediate world—which veiled a terrible or awesome reality enough to make its presence tolerable.[7]

---

[6] On this characteristic of symbols, see Paul Tillich, "Nature and Sacrament," *The Protestant Era*, trans. by James Luther Adams (Chicago, 1948), pp. 94-112.

[7] Two comprehensive interpretations of Nietzsche's aesthetic views, from differing points of view, are: Werner Brock, *Nietzsches Idee der Kultur* (Bonn, 1930); and Johannes Klein, *Die Dichtung Nietzsches* (Munich, 1936).

This gave to the symbol in both art and religion a tantalizing quality: I would want to know as much as there is to know about the Holy or the Beautiful revealed there, but I must be content with whatever I can learn through the veil of the symbol. Neither intellectualism nor moralism has been able to deal adequately with this veiled character of revelation. Since the affinity of the Holy and the Beautiful is postulated upon it, it has struck many sensitive minds.

One noteworthy element in that affinity is the way the revelation of the mystery was said to come upon the poet or prophet, through inspiration. For the ancients, this inspiration amounted to a seizure by the Holy and produced symptoms closely approximating those of intoxication—at times, in fact, it was more than mere approximation! Both poetic rapture and religious revelation were supposed to produce a certain frenzy in the agents whom the gods had selected to speak their will. The underlying motif of this notion was its realization that the worship of the Holy or of the Beautiful involved the surrender of one's own will and even of his rational processes to the overwhelming power of the divine. There was here a realization of the need for personal commitment—for letting the Holy take hold of me and carry me where it willed rather than where I willed. Once more aestheticism shows how much more deeply it has been able to deal with the transcendent Holy than either intellectualism or moralism. It is difficult to imagine an existential commitment to either a metaphysical system or an ethical code, but without existential commitment to a fascination beyond me I cannot be in relation to either the Holy or the Beautiful.

Both art and religion have sought to answer some of life's basic problems by bringing to man communion with a reality beyond his immediate knowledge. Poets and prophets have long since pointed out that these basic problems are the problems of pain and suffering, tragedy and death. The Beautiful and the Holy have so easily converged because both have been dominated by themes like pain and tragedy. Writers on the theory of dramatics have long tried to explain just why so many of the world's great plays have been tragedies. Why do men everywhere still turn to *Oedipus Tyrannus* or *Medea* and sense there a contemporary quality which they miss in even the greatest of the Greek comedies? What is it about *Hamlet* or *Lear* or *Doctor Faustus* that sets them apart from the great bulk of Elizabethan drama? The answer is a complex one, but near to the root of the matter was the statement of Nietzsche that "pain begets joy, that ecstasy may wring sounds of agony from us."[8] Any interpretation of life beyond the most naive has included somewhere the observation that there was no birth except in pain, and it has been the strength of tragedy that it brought out this insight and presented it in a manner that spoke to the universal pain and tragedy of all human existence.

This has been the theme of great art, it has also been the message of the great religious teachers. Even apart

---

[8]Friedrich Nietzsche, *The Birth of Tragedy from the Spirit of Music,* trans. by Clifton Fadiman, *The Philosophy of Nietzsche* (*Modern Library* Edition), p. 959. Further references to Nietzsche will be to the page numbers of this edition.

from the Cross, men have recognized that God crushed in order to raise up, that He weakened in order to make strong, that He killed in order to resurrect. For that reason, it has been a constant temptation in Christian thought, and especially in Christian art, to see the Cross as an exemplification of this general rule in all existence and the Crucified as the prototype of the tragic victory that would come if one heroically endured his cross till he emerged triumphant, bloody but unbowed. The offense of the Cross did not consist in its tragedy, this was its appeal also to the natural man. The Cross was foolishness to the Greeks, who knew of Oedipus, and a stumbling block to the Jews, who knew the pain of the prophets and the tears of the psalmists. This was because the Cross asserted that the tragedy of mankind could not be understood or resolved except by an act of God, and that the one unique and distinctive act of God by which this was accomplished was the life, death, and resurrection of the historical Jesus Christ. It is not offensive to be told of tragedy, it is downright thrilling to hear of heroic suffering. This elicits our interest and admiration, because we too have suffered, we hope heroically, and it is comforting to know that in our suffering we have such brilliant company. But when the gospel comes to tell us that our suffering is well deserved, and that only by the innocence of the Saviour can our guilt be removed—this is too much to take.

What has made the identification of the Holy and the Beautiful such a subtle and alluring thing was the vicarious element in any tragic drama—that I could see my sufferings in the example of another and could rather enjoy the prospect. As soon as the Cross was moved from the life of Jesus to the status of a general principle that was universally applicable, I could begin to view it objectively and yet see myself in it. This I could do best in aesthetic observation, and the identification of the Holy and the Beautiful has made such observation the essence of worship.

Such a desire to find in something outside me a principle that will explain the life within me has operated to identify the Holy and the Beautiful in another way, namely, the observation of the beauty and symmetry of nature as concrete evidence of the beauty of God. A particularly appealing version of this viewpoint has been the doctrine that the closest thing to the divine we could experience was the sense of creativity coming over us in the delicate stirrings of artistic genius or the wistful longings of sex. According to this doctrine, God was the projection of the many and complicated creativities which we experienced in observing the strivings of nature's impulses within us as well as in the external universe. Like Schopenhauer's will-to-be, this creativity was the one principle which all forms of reality shared. Each in its own way thus demonstrated and exemplified the creativity of God.[9]

The blossoming of the flowers in the spring, the color of the autumn, the poetry that comes to our lips when we are at a loss to express an emotion that has come over us, the power of music, the awe we sense in the presence of artistic masterpieces—all these were actu-

---

[9]See Tillich's polemic against what he calls "philosophy of life," *Systematic Theology*, I (Chicago, 1951), 99-100.

ally experiences of the creativity of God. God was the
supreme Artist of the universe: not so much the Archi-
teet who had designed and supervised the construction
as the Artist who took what He could get and fashioned
it into beautiful forms that could provide human life
with meaning, value, and beauty. We could participate
in the creativity of God if we learned sensitively to appreciate the gentle beauties He fashioned from the stuff
of our experience and if we shared those beauties with
others. In such an outlook, the identification of the Holy
and the Beautiful was no longer a side issue. It became
instead the formal principle of a religious faith in which
the physical universe, the moral consciousness, the joy
of begetting, and the pain of dying were all united in
one all-embracing affirmation of the creativity and the
beauty that is God.

Such an interpretation of the artistic nature of God
was possible in an effete and sophisticated culture, dis-
satisfied with the partial and inadequate answers to
life being offered by science and by material comfort.
It depended on the presence and power of a faith that
had found aesthetic expression in music, poetry, and
art. Once the faith had developed such expressions, it
became easy to equate these expressions with the faith
that produced them, and eventually to dispense with
the faith itself altogether.

Precisely here has been the danger in the study of
churchly arts like painting, music, and liturgy. One
could be so impressed with the artistic magnificence of
Christian cultural forms that the dynamic which produced these forms was entombed in the forms which

it had developed. The perfumed charm of Gregorian chant or the virile tones of the German chorale could become the indispensable condition of Christian culture, rather than one example among many examples of how the dynamic of the Christian faith can become embodied in an art form. The identification of the Holy and the Beautiful has frequently become the identification of the Holy with this Beautiful or with that, so that a particular cultural and artistic tradition was endowed with a divinity it did not have. To be sure, it was more comfortable to live with an art form than with God, and this has been the fundamental temptation of the identification of the Holy and the Beautiful—that in aesthetic rapture I had enough commitment to satisfy me, yet not so much that I lost my self-respect.

Because he was attracted to the identification of the Holy and the Beautiful for many of the reasons we have been enumerating, Friedrich Nietzsche is the thinker whose thought we shall analyze for the way he formulated this identification and the way he was compelled by his realization of the demonic in man to overthrow it.

There were many influences in the life and thought of Nietzsche that drew him to aestheticism. Not the least among these was his friendship with the German music dramatist, Richard Wagner. In his prose writings as well as in his music dramas, Wagner voiced his conviction that the basic value in life was the aesthetic, and that from the standpoint of the Beautiful the problems of life could be resolved. It was with this end in mind that Wagner evolved a new art form to replace the rather amorphous opera of France and Italy. The music drama was to be a modern, musical expression of the same ideal that had dominated the Greek tragedy. Here, through the medium of orchestral and vocal music, the artist-composer wanted to deal with the most profound problems that engaged the human spirit, believing that dramatization intensified by the emotional impact of music was the best of all possible means to present both the problems and the solution. He did not wish to compose mere allegory, in which each character would stand for a particular virtue or vice. Rather, like the Greek tragedians, he wanted to use traditional material—*Parsifal*, the *Ring*, *Lohengrin*, and *Tannhaeuser* were all based upon ancient German folklore—to highlight his highly untraditional doctrines of art, morality, and religion. The music drama was, Wagner believed, capable of expressing an answer to life's questions far superior to the answers of conventional religion or philosophy.

Through his association with Wagner, Nietzsche acquired a similar faith in art as the revealer of values beyond the reach of any other human endeavor. Gratitude to Wagner for this faith moved Nietzsche to dedicate his treatise on *The Birth of Tragedy from the Spirit of Music* to his friend, who had taught him "that art is the highest task and the proper metaphysical activity of this life, as it is understood by the man to whom, as my noble champion on this same path, I now dedicate this essay." What Koeberle has called "the glowing, sense-intoxicating, sensuous Bacchanalians of the tone colors" in Wagner's music and his "voluptuous, cloying

sensualism" were the elements of Wagner's genius that
appealed to Nietzsche, for in the frenzy of the Beautiful
he saw the highest meaning of life.[10]

Wagner's work was all the more attractive to Nietzsche because of its relation to the spirit of Greek tragedy. By training and profession, Nietzsche was a student of classical philology, and his thinking was sat-
urated with the culture of Greece. Among his colleagues
at Basel was the historian Jakob Burckhardt, author of a
monumental study of Greek cultural history, as well as
the unconventional church historian Franz Overbeck.
Their work aided and encouraged Nietzsche in his
studies of the genius of Greek tragedy. As we have seen,
a fundamental motif shaping the drama of ancient
Greece was the belief that dramatic art was a form of
worship.

The essay on *The Birth of Tragedy* was a brilliant
analysis of that belief. Nietzsche contrasted two streams
of thought in Greek culture, represented by the two gods
Apollo and Dionysus. Apollo stood for the rational, con-
templative life, the life of reason, the work of the philosopher. Dionysus symbolized vitality, intoxication,
frenzy, the work of the artist. Too much of Western culture, Nietzsche said, had been based upon the Apollonian elements of ancient Greece, and not enough upon
the Dionysian. This had given Western thought—
Nietzsche was thinking here primarily of German
philosophy in the nineteenth century—its rationalistic
character and had prevented it from dealing with those

---

[10]"Foreword" to *The Birth of Tragedy*, p. 950; Adolf Koeberle,
The Quest for Holiness, p. 7.

problems that only the *Rausch* (rapture) of the Dionysian artist could solve. As a consequence, most of the systems of thought that had been developed in the past centuries were arid, utterly devoid of the ability to enthuse and animate. Rational philosophy simply could not appeal to those stirrings of the soul which were most basic and most important. Only the artist or musician could make such an appeal. When the West had discovered this, perhaps it would forsake its philosophies and theologies and seek the transcendent Holy where it was to be found, in the beauty and pathos of art.[11]

Contributing to Nietzsche's sympathy for the aesthetic doctrines of Wagner and the aesthetic propensities of Greek culture was his own personal disposition and sensitivity. All his life Nietzsche was a hypochondriac, and in his later years this hypochondria was intensified. He tried changes of climate, medicines of all kinds, fantastic diets, to alleviate his pain and depression. But none of them helped. The reason was that the root of his trouble was not physical but spiritual, as was to be shown by his ultimate collapse. The only relief he could find for his suffering was in music and art. He spoke in *Ecce Homo* of the "necessity for stilling a feeling of emptiness and hunger, through the medium of a narcotic art."[12] There the poor sufferer found release in the contemplation of the Beautiful.

---

[11]Nietzsche looked forward to a relation of Apollonian and Dionysian in which the Apollonian "begins to talk with Dionysian wisdom. . . .[and] finally speaks the language of Dionysus," *The Birth of Tragedy*, p. 1071.

[12]*Ecce Homo*, p. 881.

But Nietzsche insisted that this contemplation of the Beautiful had to be existential, or, as he put it, that it dare not be from the standpoint of a spectator. He was correct in this insistence. No relation with the Holy based on detached observation would satisfy man's need for fellowship. This very insistence brought on his downfall, too. Once he had involved himself in an existential encounter with the Holy, which, like Don Juan, he sought in the Beautiful, there was no retreating and no relenting until the power of the Holy which had been unleashed had overwhelmed him. This was no mild flirtation but an overwhelming passion, and once the passion had turned to hatred, this too was existential. The criticism Nietzsche leveled at aestheticism was not a mild, dispassionate evaluation, but a disavowal fully as intense as his love for aestheticism had been.

One of the forces that brought Nietzsche to his rejection of the identification of the Holy and the Beautiful was the symbol he himself had used to exemplify his scorn for all conventional values, the superman. Nietzsche's ideal superman was the goal for which all man's evolution had been striving, for man had to become more than he was. As man represented a triumph over the animals, so superman was a triumph over men as they had developed so far. None of the usual standards that were applied to human conduct and thought could be used to judge the superman. Ethics was the device that dominant groups in society had used to enforce their will upon their fellows. It was necessary so long as men continued to act like sheep. But this *Herdenmoral*, the morality of the herd, had to give way to the *Herrenmoral*, the morality of the masters, the ethic of the superman.[13] Since it was for the production of the superman that all things existed and since he represented not only the climax but also the goal of all human development, it followed that what served him was good and what stood in his way was bad, regardless of any other standard or criterion. Like goodness, truth also had to be recast for the superman: the True was what superman said was true.

By this assertion of the superiority of superman to all conventional norms of value, Nietzsche expressed his contempt for what he regarded as Christian submissiveness and negation. He accused Christianity of crushing every positive and vigorous assertion in the European mind and of substituting for the virility of the human spirit a false notion of self-denial. The superman was to overcome Christianity's strictures upon self-assertion and to break the bonds that had shackled European thought and culture since Christianity became the dominant religion. What Nietzsche did not immediately realize when he embarked upon this course of thought was that if the superman was to call into question every traditional value in the name of his self-assertive creativity, then that creativity itself would have to be called very seriously into question. He had regarded art as the best expression of man's creative urge, and in the essay on *The Birth of Tragedy* he had glorified art as the proper articulation of man as he was and should be. But he could not finish his rejection of traditional

---

[13]On the two types of morality, cf., among other passages, *Beyond Good and Evil*, pp. 578 ff.

criteria of the Good and the True until he had over-
thrown traditional criteria of the Beautiful as well. His
retractions of previous views in *Ecce Homo* showed
that he was willing to go this far, but soon thereafter his
mind collapsed. All values had crumbled—devaluated.
Not even the Beautiful remained, nor even the Holy.

For God was dead![14] This was the message of Zarathustra, that the Holy to which men had looked in
times of sorrow was unworthy of their faith and devotion. The superman could no more worship God than
he could revere other conventions of truth or of goodness. Prometheus, whom Nietzsche thought of as the ex-
emplar of the superman, began with opposition to customs, but this opposition ran headlong into the hate of
the gods, who bound him with chains to a rock in the
Caucasus. If the superman was to survive, eventually
he had to kill God.

This was no poetic device on the part of Nietzsche,
but a profound realization of the deepest meaning in
the doctrine of the sovereignty of God. If what Christianity said about the lordship of Christ was true, there
could be no superman. All his life Nietzsche was
haunted by the figure of Christ, and even when he
spurned Christ he did so in an existential, even religious
way. With a penetration sadly lacking among many
theologians of the time, Nietzsche saw the fuller implications of the figure of Jesus. Jesus was not an example of what man could be if he cultivated the moral
will in his innermost being. Nor was he the highest attainable stage in the evolution of man. His difference

[14]"Prologue" to *Thus Spake Zarathustra*, p. 6

from men was not quantitative but qualitative. The holiness of Christ did not challenge men to improve themselves, it demanded that they repent. Christ represented God's judgment upon every human attempt at self-improvement, He was the despair of any theory that pointed men beyond themselves to a divine congruent with their innermost longings. He was indeed the devalnation of all values that the superman had preached, but He was that because the Holy stood in judgment upon any of the values men had projected and all the systems they had devised.

While some theologians were proclaiming that the kingdom of God could be discovered and brought to fruition by the moral improvement of man, Nietzsche saw that to accomplish his program he had to be rid of the damning presence of the Christ. There could be no compromise with the God who was the Father of the Lord Jesus Christ, no compromise and no barter. The claim that He laid upon men as their Creator and Lord had to be swept aside before the superman could emerge. Thus did Nietzsche perceive that the Holy was no mere value to be aimed for and hoped for—neither the True nor the Good nor even the Beautiful. With any of these a man could deal, and superman could make all of them serve his purposes. But the Holy was jealous and would brook no opposition, so God had to die before superman could be born.[15]

After such an existential realization of the power and awe of the Holy, Nietzsche could not think of equating

---

[15]"Away from God and gods did this will allure me; what woul'' there be to create if there were—gods!" *Ibid.*, p. 92.

Him with the gentle beauties of nature. The activity of God was much too furious for that. It was the sheerest romanticism, Nietzsche soon learned, to attempt to trap the Holy in the beauties of nature. If there was a creativity of God in the universe, there was as certainly a destructivity of God. If we were to ascribe to God all the loveliness and tenderness in nature, sex, society, and art, we surely had to make Him responsible for all the cruelty and pain and death that asserted themselves in these areas. If there was something in God that made the rose and the sunset, there was also something that made the cobra and the tornado. If God was beautiful, He was also ugly; if He was the principle of life, He also had to be the principle of death.

Nietzsche's atheism sprang, then, from an awareness of the God against whom he had revolted. He knew that the Holy was a force no man could control, that God was neither lovely nor congenial. God was not a kindly old man who gently nodded at the blunders of His children or grandchildren and who could be appeased with a few childish presents. There was nothing beautiful or tender about the God who could and did forsake the Crucified and plunge Him into the damnation of being cut off from the divine life. God was a consuming fire and a raging torrent. Whom but God did man meet in the hour of death, awaiting him not with comfort or kindness, but with holiness and judgment? Nietzsche's understanding of the Holy was far more profound than some so-called Christian doctrines of God, for it broke completely with any identification of the Holy and the categories of human value.

Nietzsche's doctrine of man also helped him to overcome the equation of the Holy and the Beautiful. The
essence of human nature Nietzsche saw in the will-to-
power, of which all human strivings and values were
merely expressions. Men wanted to have others believe
that they were following a particular course for high
and noble motives, but they were actually asserting a ,
will-to-power. This will-to-power could easily use the
Beautiful as a shield for its demonic urgings. Precisely
this happened when the Beautiful was identified with
the Holy. Such an identification, stripped of all its
pretensions, was an expression of the will-to-power and
of the drive for control over the Holy. Fundamentally,
the will-to-power meant that man would stand for no
challenge to his survival or nobility on the part of anything or anyone, not even God. Paradoxically, he would
rather die than let anything stand in his way. And he
would use every possible device to ward off the Holy
that sought his life.[16]

Nietzsche perceived in later years how demonic the
identification of the Holy and the Beautiful could be.
It could act as a mask for the will-to-power. With the
disarming honesty that was at once his greatest strength
and his great weakness, Nietzsche confessed to the will-
to-power that had been at work in his advocacy of this
identification. But it was too late for him to return. He

---

[16]Nietzsche's concept of will-to-power is briefly summarized in a
work published shortly after his death, Rudolf Eisler, *Nietzsches Er-
kenntnistheorie und Metaphysik* (Leipzig, 1902), pp, 77-117; see also
the interesting discussion from the Hitler period, Walther Spethmann,
Der Begriff des Herrentums bei Nietzsche (Berlin, 1935), pp. 59-62
and *passim*.

had systematically brought down every prop upon which men build their lives. Morality had collapsed under his criticism, philosophy had crumbled, even art had deserted him. Robbed of all the resources for consolation and comfort that sustained other men in their age and weakness, obsessed with a Holy that would not leave him and yet would not accept him, Nietzsche slipped away into the darkness and silence of insanity, where he died.

Of the three values we have been discussing here, the Beautiful has been the most attractive, and the identification of the Holy and the Beautiful the most subtle. Sane men have found it difficult to go back on their intellectual training, even harder to reject their ethical inclinations, almost impossible to give up their dream of beauty. Like Helen in *Faust*, it has risen up to inspire them and to fire their imagination. It took an insane man, lonely, embittered, and frustrated, to spurn even this last comfort. Nietzsche was insane enough to deny himself everything that might have made his life meaningful.

This is what makes this madman a "fool for Christ," though he refused to be called a Christian.[17] He took seriously the Christian assertion that without Christ life was meaningless and without God life was hopeless. He came to know that all the identifications of the Holy with the True or the Good or even the Beautiful were

---

[17]Thus he termed himself "the severest opponent of Christianity," *Ecce Homo*, p. 829; and "Antichrist," *ibid.*, p. 858. Perhaps the most penetrating discussion of Nietzsche's hostility and yet affinity for Christianity is Karl Jaspers, *Nietzsche und das Christentum* (2nd ed.; Munich, 1952).

narcotic self-deceptions by which men vainly tried to dull the horrible sense of loneliness and defeat that dogged their every step. Here was one man who was willing to see it through all the way regardless of consequences. After casting aside other values, he was drawn to the Beautiful as an explanation of the meaning of life. Yet eventually he left that behind, too, and faced the nakedness of God alone. In this he stood in ' marked contrast to many Christians of that day and this, who have not let God interfere with any of their values, but have regarded Him as the fulfillment of all their fondest dreams and their tenderest longings. Truth did not point to God, Goodness did not lead to God, Beauty did not speak of God: all this Nietzsche realized during those ten dark years when he lived in the madness of the Holy.

THE BEAUTY OF HOLINESS

BACH

In this concluding essay we shall deal positively with the third of the values with which at various times the Holy has been identified. On the basis of the aesthetic ideals of Nietzsche we have sought to show that an attempt to find the Holy in the subtle stirrings of the Beautiful ends in the maddening realization that the Holy refuses to be taken captive in the Beautiful. Now we want to look at the possibility of a positive relation between the Holy and the Beautiful, in which the priority of the Holy would itself be productive of an interpretation of the nature of the Beautiful. As a case study we shall use Johann Sebastian Bach, a man of explicit Christian faith and acknowledged artistic competence, in whose thought and work we shall examine the connections between these two areas.[1]

We prefaced our presentation of Paul's conception of truth in Christ with a discussion of the viewpoint which

---

[1]An excellent survey of Bach's significance is Hans Besch, *Johann Sebastian Bach, Froemmigkeit und Glaube*, I (Guetersloh, 1938); as my discussion indicates, I find myself somewhat in disagreement with Besch, and in agreement more with Spitta, on Bach's relation to the *Zeitgeist*.

made a Christ of truth, and our presentation of Luther's
thought about the goodness of God with an analysis of
the approach that made a god of goodness. A parallel
situation is present here. The antipode of the beauty of
holiness is the holiness of beauty, an interpretation of
the nature of the Beautiful that sees it not in a derivative
relation to the Holy but as a genus of holiness in and of
itself. The historic significance of Bach will become
clearer against the background of such a theory of "the
holiness of beauty."

This theory was indeed current in Bach's world, and
he met with it in his own contemporaries. Thanks to
recent trends in theology, studies of the Enlightenment
have suffered a slight setback since the work of Dilthey
and Troeltsch. We can say nevertheless that in the
movement of thought loosely termed the Enlightenment
there were many who were inclined to aestheticism. It
would not be accurate to designate this strain as a universal one in Enlightenment thought. In fact, an inci-
dent in Bach's own life demonstrates the inaccuracy of
such an interpretation. In the years 1734 to 1736 Bach
came into serious conflict with Johann August Ernesti,
who had been chosen as rector of the Thomas School in
Leipzig. Ernesti was one of the founders of the science
of biblical criticism and as such an important figure in
the history of Enlightenment theology, usually linked
with Michaelis and Semler. As rector of the Thomas
School, he displayed a hearty lack of sympathy with
music in general, with church music in particular, and
most particularly of all with Bach's brand of church
music. His concern was with the practical aspects of

life and religion, and in this he was the spokesman for many Rationalists of the time. They wanted only those ideas and forms to prevail in the church that were immediately applicable to the moral needs of the people. They had no interest in art for art's sake or beauty for beauty's sake.[2]

Bach's conflict with this Philistinism in Enlightenment thought as represented by Ernesti was, therefore, a defense of the legitimacy of the Beautiful in the church. It serves to illustrate the observation that by no means all the theologians of the Enlightenment were inclined to aestheticism. At almost the same time, Bach was confronting in Johann Adolf Scheibe the more prevalent aesthetic theory of the Enlightenment. Scheibe's aesthetic theory, dependent upon the philosophy of Gottsched, was instrumental in the formation of the musical theories of Lessing and thus came ultimately to influence the greatest aesthete of them all, Goethe. Characteristic of this aestheticism in Enlightenment thought was that sensitivity to which Lessing gave the name *empfindsam*, his translation of the French *sentimental*. It was aimed at the transformation of the human spirit by ennobling the senses, and it sought to ennoble the senses by exposing them to what was high and noble in the artistic productions of other human spirits.[3]

Research into the Enlightenment theory of education from this point of view has not gone very far, but there are strong indications that Enlightenment aestheticism

[2]Robert Stevenson, "Bach's Quarrel with the Rector of St. Thomas School," *Anglican Theological Review*, XXXIII (1951), 219-230.

[3]Fred Hamel, *Johann Sebastian Bach. Geistige Welt* (Goettingen, 1951), pp. 158-169, on Scheibe's relation to Gottsched and to Bach.

may have been strongly pedagogical in its motivation.
It tended to replace older methods of indoctrination and
moral instruction with a program of moral training in
which the arts were to make a definite contribution.
Combined with a resurgence of Renaissance classical
humanism and the beginnings of German national consciousness in literature and the arts, Enlightenment
educational theory was able to make use of the finest
artistic productions of antiquity and of the best being
produced in its own time for molding character through
art. The early appearance of these features in the German Enlightenment make somewhat suspect the rather
sharp distinction made by many histories of German
literature and music between the Enlightenment and
the "Romantic period," this latter seen as essentially a
protest against Enlightenment Rationalism. There is
much to be said for an interpretation of the Enlightenment that sees Rationalism and Romanticism in it side
by side almost from the beginning of the eighteenth
century, at least in Germany.

Whatever one may term it, there was a powerful climate of opinion in Bach's day that assigned to the arts
a prominent function in the shaping of human thought
and life. Not a little of modern aestheticism can be
traced to the idea so prevalent in the Enlightenment
that the Beautiful had power to transform men by its
sheer beauty. According to this idea, there was an almost mathematical symmetry in the human psyche that
needed to be related to some symmetry outside it. The
arts and the sciences were both charged with the responsibility of discovering this symmetry and making

it available. Many Enlightenment thinkers shared with the ancient Greeks the notion that mathematical symbols were somehow possessed of a reality all their own, a notion that became fundamental in the metaphysics of Christian Wolff. Since mathematics was basic to so much in art, whether through rhythm or proportion or some similar mathematical relation, Enlightenment thinkers made use of the arts as means to relate the symmetry of the external world, the world of sense and experience, to the symmetry already present a priori, independent of and antecedent to all experience, in the human mind itself.

This sense of symmetry and balance innate in the human mind was, in turn, a means by which man could be motivated in the direction of proper conduct. He had within himself the awareness of natural law and of the morally Good, which enabled him both to know and to will that which was ethically desirable. To this capacity within man, then, the arts could make their appeal by teaching man the good, balanced, symmetrical, proportioned, and rhythmical life. Some historians of the period have produced interesting analyses of the minuet and the gavotte, of both their music and their steps, as exemplifications of the graceful and the balanced in much of the Enlightenment. These dances symbolized the belief shared by many Enlightenment thinkers that the proper application of the arts to the human spirit would bring it into harmony with itself and with the world. Music and all the arts had charms to soothe the savage breast and perhaps even to civilize it. Thus beauty had acquired a certain holiness of its own, and a power to transform or to consecrate its patrons and to give them the Holy by teaching them to know the Beautiful.[4]

Bach's relation to this climate of opinion hangs together with the larger question of his relation to the eighteenth century generally. On this larger question the brilliant and exceedingly helpful study of Bach by Albert Schweitzer offers some rather puzzling answers. Schweitzer's treatment of the question of how Bach was related to his time is set into the context of his introductory discussion of the difference between "objective" and "subjective" music. By "subjective music Schweitzer designates that which reflects the inner workings of the mind of the composer, by "objective" music that which speaks more for the time in which the composer lived than for his own self-consciousness. Proceeding on the basis of this distinction, Schweitzer suggests that Bach was an objective musician and in many ways the spokesman of his time. "To give his true biography is to exhibit the nature and the unfolding of German art. . . . This genius was not an individual, but a collective soul. . . . The history of this epoch is the history of that culminating spirit, as it was before it objectivated itself in a single personality."[5]

The thesis has something to be said for it on the question of musical technique. Still the designation of Bach as the objectivation of the spirit of his time does not

[4]Ernst Cassirer, *The Philosophy of the Enlightenment*, pp. 275-360; R. L. Brett, *The Third Earl of Shaftesbury* (London, 1951), pp. 123-144.

[5]Albert Schweitzer, J. S. Bach, trans. by Ernest Newman (London, 1938), I, 3-4.

take the full measure of the wide cleft between Bach's theological orientation and that of the Enlightenment, and therefore of the vast difference between his aesthetic principle and those of his contemporaries, which we have just sketched. The question of Bach's relation to the Enlightenment has been a central issue of research on Bach, after earlier scholars like Spitta had carefully delineated his debt to the Pietism and Orthodoxy of his immediate past. On the basis of this research, it is now possible to evaluate the total problem of Bach's position amid the currents of thought in the eighteenth century.[6]

It seems clear that while Bach was influenced in his musical forms by certain aspects of the Enlightenment and while the texts of his cantatas did reflect Enlightenment thinking, his fundamental theological orientation was almost completely out of harmony with the basic metaphysical and theological presuppositions of the German *Aufklaerung*. While the Enlightenment had as its avowed purpose the reduction of the content of Christian faith and doctrine to a certain irreducible minimum of common sense, Bach's understanding of the meaning of human life was rooted in the theological conviction that the minimum of Christian faith was the givenness of revelation in Christ. The motif of Enlightenment theology was the generally religious, the motif of Bach's theology was the specifically Christian. One student of Bach has summarized the contrast in this

---

[6]E. Segnitz, "Bach und der Pietismus," *Allgemeine Musikalische Zeitschrift*, XXXVI (1909), Nr. 28-31; Ph. Spitta, *J. S. Bach* (3rd ed.; Leipzig, 1921), II, 479; Walter Blankenburg, "Bach und die Aufklaerung," *Bach-Gedenkschrift*, ed. by Karl Matthaei (Zurich, 1950).

way: "I have yet to find in Bach's confessions, either by word or by the implications of his life or in the content of his music, any concern for religion save as that word meant to him the common faith of his people and church and time. The good city of the consummation toward which his soul pressed was not Parnassus but Jerusalem; the songs which drew from him the wonderfully sweet and devout arias of the cantatas were not the songs of Pan but the songs of Zion; the spirit whose might he evoked in his labors was not the Goethean spirit of the Cosmos but the Holy Ghost of his stout faith; the river at whose waters he 'sings the song of Zion in a strange land' is not the mythological Lethe but the historical Babylon."[7]

Because it was with these things that Bach's piety dealt and to these things that his faith looked, he was vastly out of sympathy with the religiosity of the Enlightenment and with the theology which that religiosity produced. Study of Bach's library has shown that the sources of his theological insight were not contemporary to him but were largely from the periods preceding the years of his mature productivity.[8] Significantly, Bach was one generation older than Ernesti. The sources of his conflict with men like Ernesti are, then, to be sought not merely in personal factors, though these were certainly present, but also in the diametrically opposed conceptions of the Christian faith held by Bach on the one hand and many of his contemporaries on the other hand.

---

[7]Joseph Sittler in *The Cresset* (April, 1943), p. 23.
[8]Hans Preusz, "Bachs Bibliothek," *Festgabe fuer Theodor Zahn* (Leipzig, 1928), pp. 105-129.

Bach was not carried along by the leading theological currents of his time; on the contrary, he was one of the last spirits in the middle of the eighteenth century to swim against those currents.

As this was true of his theological outlook generally, so it was true also and especially of his attitude toward the relation between the Holy and the Beautiful. Bach did not believe, with much of the Enlightenment, that the natural mind of itself possessed potentialities for self-realization which rationality and the arts could call forth. Rather he agreed with the words of Lazarus Spengler, to which he wrote a magnificent chorale prelude, "All mankind fell in Adam's fall." Since this was the condition of the natural human mind, no exposure to any of the arts, however beautiful, could be expected to change man. In the words of Cantata 18, Bach's faith declared: "My soul's treasure is the Word of God."⁹ His whole life and work were a living testimony to his conviction that man could not live by bread or by beauty, but only by the Word that proceeded from the mouth of God. Beauty was demonic if it was not subordinated to the speaking of God. It was not the pathway to the Eternal or the road to joy. True contact with the Eternal, abiding joy, and therefore the only Beautiful with which Bach wanted to live was to be had in the Holy. Cantata 4 voiced his faith: "Christ Jesus lay in death's strong bands, for our offenses given; but now at God's right hand He stands and brings us life from heaven. *Therefore* let us joyful be and sing

---

⁹*Orgelbuechlein*, V, 13; Cantata 18, "Gleichwie der Regen und Schnee von Himmel faellt," based on Isaiah 55.

to God right thankfully loud songs of hallelujah." It is symbolic of Bach's view of the relation between the Holy and the Beautiful that Cantata 1 was an adaptation of Philipp Nicolai's "How lovely shines the morning star."[10]

There was one figure among Bach's immediate contemporaries with whom his outlook offers valuable analogies, the much neglected theologian Valentin Ernst Loescher, who died one year before Bach. Like Bach, Loescher appeared anomalous in the midst of the eighteenth-century German Protestant *Zeitgeist* (the mood of the times), for he could not be classified or identified with any of the major parties in the church of the time.[11] In contrast to Orthodoxy, Pietism, and the Enlightenment, all of which had neglected the full meaning of the church, both Loescher and Bach identified themselves with the church and with the Holy represented there. They refused to follow the True for its own sake, be it ever so orthodox; or the Good for its own sake, be it ever so moral; or the Beautiful for its own sake, be it ever so enlightened. It was the genius of Loescher that amid both Orthodoxy and Pietism he was able in the name of the Holy to cultivate both the True and the Good. Similarly, it was the genius of Bach

---

[10]Cantata 4, "Christ lag in Todesbanden"; Cantata 1, "Wie schoen leuchtet der Morgenstern." Cf. the comments of Friedrich Smend (ed.), Joh. Seb. Bach, *Kirchen-Kantaten* (2nd ed.; Berlin, 1950), I, 14-17.

[11]Moritz von Engelhardt has summarized Loescher's position trenchantly: "Heretofore [in Orthodoxy] the leaders of the Church had forgotten the Church or the communion of saints because of pure doctrine; now [in Pietism] they forgot the Church in their zeal for a Christian life. They were both unchurchly," *Valentin Ernst Loescher nach seinem Leben und Wirken* (2nd ed.; Stuttgart, 1856), p. 25.

that though he refused to join in the idolatrous quest
for the eternal feminine in the Beautiful, he found in
his service to the Holy a new and more profound conception of the Beautiful as well. It is with this conception of the Beautiful that we shall deal by positing
several dialectical propositions aimed at summarizing
Bach's view of Christian art.[12]

The first proposition illustrated by the work of Bach
is this: *According to Bach, the highest activity of the
human spirit was the praise of God, but such praise involved the total activity of the spirit.* The highest possible activity to which the human spirit might ascend
was the praise of God. When, in the ancient canon of
the mass, the officiant called out, "Lift up your hearts,"
the only possible answer was, "We lift them up unto
the Lord." Any object of the uplifted heart short of the
Lord himself was unworthy of the best aspirations of
a human spirit created and recreated by the Creator
Spirit. Bach's setting of the aria "Laudamus Te" in the
Mass in B Minor bespeaks the high and holy privilege
he felt (apparently not shared by those sopranos who
handle it as though it were opera) in having the opportunity to praise and bless the Almighty. It would be
worth while to analyze all of Bach's settings for the
"Gloria Patri" and the "Gloria in excelsis" to document

[12]I presented these theses in a lecture entitled "Idolatry, Iconoclasm, and the Incarnation," delivered in connection with the ex-
hibition of "Living Christian Art" at Concordia Seminary, Saint Louis,
in the fall of 1953. They were based partly on a study of John of
Damascus (see note 18 below), partly on an analysis of Bach, with
the aid of Andre Pirro, *L'esthetique de J. S. Bach* (Paris, 1907),
which analyzes Bach's work more philosophically than the present
essay, but has made a substantial contribution to this discussion.

the exhilaration evident there as the composer raised his
voice in the full-throated praise of God. In spite of
criticisms which his contemporaries and some fastidious persons since have voiced against it, the same overpowering joy was at work in Bach's slightly rococo
chorale prelude, "In dulci jubilo," and it throbbed in
the wild cadences of Cantata 30: "Freue dich, freue,
erloeste Schar." Such adoration of the Holy was the
most exalted expression of the human spirit.[18]

Yet the adoration of the Holy was the adoration of
Him who was Creator, Redeemer, and Lord of all life,
and it therefore involved the total creative activity of
the spirit. It was not merely the accidents of his economic status that compelled Bach to compose other
music than church music. There was a direct relation
between "sacred" and "secular" music in Bach's work,
and not only in the fact that he used some secular
themes later on in his sacred compositions and vice
versa—though this factor is itself worthy of note. If
it was the privilege of the composer's spirit to praise
God, he could do so also when he was not composing
for the church. Bach's attitude toward his craft as an
organ builder was also indicative of his conviction that
the performance of a God-pleasing vocation was the
service of God, even without chorales. There is a certain
kind of theologism among some Bach-worshipers which
laments the fact that he felt compelled to compose
nonchurchly music.

This approach also expresses itself in a certain con-

---

[18]Cf. Smend, *Kirchen-Kantaten,* V, 18, 25, on Cantata 30 and its
relation to Bach's "secular" works.

descension toward Mozart, to say nothing of Wagner, rather like refusing to appreciate *Oedipus Tyrannus* simply because Oedipus was not crucified at the end. Entirely apart from questions of taste, such an approach is also a short-circuiting of the full nature of service to the Holy. The Holy whom the Christian faith worships in the beauty of holiness is not limited to any single "sacred" area of life, but is the all-pervading and all-ruling Holy One, the Maker of heaven and earth, the Saviour of all men, the Spirit who makes us completely His own. Thus he who would adore the Holy must bring to that adoration all the functionings of his mind and heart, including the secular functionings. The Bach of the concertos was not "too secular." He was a sort of "baptized Mozart," bringing secular composition, too, into the service of Christ the King and sanctifying all beauty, this beauty included, by a single-minded devotion to the Holy even, and especially, in "secular" culture.

This problem involves a basic issue in the theological analysis of culture. Partly because of the influence of scholasticism, many Christian interpretations of culture have regarded only that culture as Christian which adapted the best in the realm of the True and the Beautiful to the purposes of the church in Gothic, Gregorian, and the *Summa* of Aquinas. Surely no Christian involvement with culture can be complete without some such adaptation. Yet there is another task in the Christian interpretation of culture that the church has not done as well, but that nevertheless remains equally important. That is the penetration of secular culture: re-

leasing architects to build skyscrapers as well as cathe-
drals to the honor of Christ, teaching musicians to
compose string quartets as well as masses in pursuit
of their Christian calling, and creating lay philosophers
who are not interested in being theologians junior grade
but honest philosophers to the greater glory of God.[14]
A truly theonomous cultural life would be one in which
precisely these "secular activities" would become part
of the service of God, as they did in Bach.

An exposure to the dainty filigrees of the music re-
corded by Pablo Casals and his group at the 1950 Bach
Festival makes one appreciate all the more the delicate
artistry in much of Bach's sacred music, for all the
world like the finest lace—so transparent that it seems
to lack substance, yet so intricately woven that it pos-
sesses amazing strength. Similarly, observation of Bach's
craftsmanship in the use of cello and violone, now replaced by the contrabass, in the work of Casals and his
festival group helps one to appreciate the function of
these instruments, especially of the contrabass, in current editions of the *Mass:* in the opening "Kyrie," in the
bass quarter-notes throughout the opening chorus of the
"Credo," in the cello and bass accompaniment for the
"Confiteor" and the "Hosanna," in the solemn basses
during the "Sanctus." Such technique was itself a form
of divine service, whether it came in the *Mass* or in
one of the suites or in the *Musikalisches Opfer,* or even

---

[14]In an interesting aside on the significance for Bach of the Orthodox idea that inspiration reached the mouth, tongue, and hands of the
biblical writers, Besch comments: "For an organist reared in Orthodoxy, the fact that the hands, too, are in the service of God gives
ultimate meaning and adornment to his calling," op. *cit.,* p. 239.

in the delightful harpsichord and cello variations of the *Erbauliche Gedanken eines Tabakrauchers!* To paraphrase a remark of Werner Elert, written in a different context, whoever cannot appreciate such joy and sheer zest of living had better see whether his religion is derived from the New Testament or the Koran.[15] Spitta may think that Cantata 176, "Es ist ein trotzig un'd versagt Ding," sounds too much like a gavotte, but it was the expression of a spirit that dedicated even its humor to the adoration of the Holy. The highest activity of the human spirit was the praise of God, but such praise involved the total activity of the spirit.[16]

A second thesis implicit in Bach's work is this: *As the praise of the Eternal God, Christian art was an expression of boundless freedom; but as the praise of the God who had limited himself in the Incarnation, it bound itself to form.* The conception of art as freedom and release from the bonds of finiteness was an ancient one, found in the Greek view of the artist as a man set apart from the ordinary limitations of human life. Often in art the soul athirst for the Eternal has sought to find the consummation that was denied it elsewhere, and so through the history of art there runs the quest for the aesthetic absolute. Perhaps no one has described this striving for the absolute in more vital terms than Oswald Spengler in his discussion of the Faustian element in Western thought. Like Faust, the striving has also been predestined to damnation, as we saw in the case of Nietzsche. Therefore artists have had to content them-

---

[15]Werner Elert, *Morphologie des Luthertums*, I, 62.
[16]On Cantata 176, see Smend, *Kirchen-Kantaten*, II, 19-20.

selves with the realization that they would always be thrown back by the limitations of their finite existence. Thus Wagner defined the artist's task: "In truth the greatness of the poet can be best measured by what he refrains from saying, in order to let the inexpressible speak to us in secrecy."[17]

Artists have had to limit themselves because they were finite and because the matters they described were finite, too. But the Christian artist has not dealt only with the finite and the temporal. He has been a citizen of the eternal city, and he praised a God who was almighty and everlasting. It would seem therefore that he of all artists could be liberated from this finiteness which so easily besets us and be free to soar unfettered and unbounded in the timeless and spaceless realms of the absolute. In a sense, it is true that Christian art has been an expression of boundless freedom, for it has been the worship of the eternal God, not of idols. Thus Christian artists have succeeded in creating beauties that seemed not of this mortal realm. There are times when Palestrina can carry one at least to the very edge of this bounded being. There are colors in the windows of Chartres, recently made available in remarkable reproductions, before which one could fairly weep. The antiphons in Bach's setting of the "Sanctus" seem not only to fill the earth and the heavens with the glory of God, as the text declares, but to go beyond their periphery into the very presence of the Almighty. One would have himself to be made of stone or plaster not to respond with some such sensation to the master-

---

[17]Quoted in Schweitzer, op. cit., II, 16.

pieces of Michelangelo, as reproduced on film in *The Titan*. Christian art has indeed bespoken a boundless freedom.

But it has done so by voluntarily binding itself to form. The God whom Christian faith worshiped and Christian art adored has not been some Timeless who lived in endless self-contemplation as the unmoved prime mover, but the Holy who was available within our bounded existence through the boundedness of Jesus of Nazareth. Christian art has concerned itself with the absolute and the Eternal not as He was in himself—for He is a consuming fire—but as He had revealed himself in Jesus the Christ. The time-shattering strains of Palestrina's "Adoramus te" become meaningful and complete only in the "quia per sanctam Tuam crucem redemisti mundum." Christian plastic art has had to fear no anthropomorphism in its depictions of the Eternal, for it has faced the Incarnate. If anything, its problem has been to be sure to take the Incarnation seriously enough, setting it into dialectical relation to those glimpses of the Eternal which were granted it. Bach's "Pleni sunt coeli" was followed by one of the loveliest and most plaintive tenor arias of all, "Benedictus qui venit in nomine Domini." The canonic duet, "Et in unum Dominum Jesum Christum" was followed by one of Bach's best step-motifs, "Et incarnatus est," with the descent of the Infinite into the finiteness of our flesh. This combination of the boundless freedom of the Eternal with the boundedness of the Incarnate was perhaps nowhere more evident than in the Christmas oratorio.

Bach scholars have sought in various ways to explain this combination of freedom and self-limitation. Thus the critic von Luepke declared: "Bach has at present a Janus head; one face looking back to the epoch of formal architectonic structure, the other turned toward the future—toward the freest subjectivity of inward speech." Yet if one comes seriously to terms with the claim of the Christian faith that the Boundless One has come among us in the bound form of a servant, then Christian art must do both these things simultaneously. Despite the polemic of nineteenth-century historical criticism against the so-called "Byzantine Christ," some of the best icons were more successful in this task than their critics, whether of the eighth or the nineteenth century.[18] The same attempt was clearly present in the work of Bach. As the praise of the Eternal God his art was an expression of boundless freedom, but as the praise of the God who had limited himself in the Incarnation it bound itself to form.

A third generalization suggested by the music of Bach, and particularly by the *Mass*, is this: *As the medium of a historical faith, Christian art had to be cast in terms of the historical repository of its tradition; but as an expression of faith in the living God, it had to be relevant and contemporary in its use of this repository.* Bach's setting of the Nicene Creed in the *Mass* is an illustration of this thesis. The so-called Nicene Creed might well be termed the most authentic piece of tradition in Christendom, in the sense that, despite the desig-

---

[18]Cf. Karl Schwarzlose, *Der Bilderstreit* (Gotha, 1890), pp. 174-184 on Theodore of Studion; pp. 188-200 on John of Damascus.

nation "ecumenical creeds," it is the only creedal formulation which, in various forms, has been used liturgically and accepted dogmatically by both Eastern and Western churches. It has been a criterion of orthodoxy for a millennium and a half, and it is still recited by the faithful all over the world and all over the church. Around this creed and others, many theological classics have been written—Calvin's *Institutes*, the confession of Mogilas, the *Credo* of Barth. The creeds form a basic element in the theological tradition, and of them the Nicene is most hallowed by traditional and ecumenical usage.

It is this creed that Bach used in the *Mass*, as the canon of the mass prescribed. Opinions vary as to its adaptability. Schweitzer comments: "The *Symbolum Nicaenum* is a hard nut for a composer to crack. If ever there was a text put together without any idea of its being set to music it is this, in which the Greek theologians have laid down their correct and dry formulas for the conception of the godhead of Christ. In no mass has the difficulty of writing music for the *Credo* been so completely overcome as in this of Bach's." In keeping with his attitude toward classical Christology as the "graveclothes" of the historical Jesus, Schweitzer would seem to hold that the Nicene Creed with its elaborate second article does not easily lend itself to musical adaptation. Calvin would appear to have been more accurate in his evaluation of the Nicene Creed: "It is, you see, more a hymn suited for singing than a formula of confession." Schweitzer himself seems to suggest this when he says a little later: "Bach thus proves that the dogma can be expressed much more clearly and satisfactorily in music than in verbal formulae. His exegesis of these passages in the Nicene Creed has resolved the disputes that excited the Eastern world for many generations and finally delivered it over to Islam; his presentation of the dogma even makes it acceptable to minds for which dogma has no attraction."[19]

A look at what Bach did with the most controversial elements in the Nicene Creed will illustrate this point. The two most highly controverted words in the Latin text of the Creed were the "consubstantialem" in the second article and the "filioque" in the third article. The dogmatician would have been tempted to concentrate his attention upon these two, upon the *homoousios* (identity of essence) to prove his orthodoxy against the Arians and Socinians, and upon the "filioque" to prove his catholicity against the East. In his setting of the Creed, Bach all but ignored both these phrases. The duet, "Et in unum Dominum" has been described by commentators as programmatic, showing how the Son proceeds from the Father, and this may be correct. It is interesting to note that in one of the repetitions of the text, the words read: "Deum verum de Deo vero, per quem omnia facta sunt," thus altogether skipping the "consubstantialem." With the "filioque," Bach was almost as cavalier, except that he accompanied the bass solo setting of this section with an *oboe d'amore* that made the dogma fairly lilt.

---

[19]Schweitzer, op. *cit.*, II, 317-319; John Calvin, "Adversus Petri Caroli Calumnias," *Opera, Corpus Reformatorum* (Braunschweig, 1869 ff.), VII, 316.

Now it cannot be denied that Bach was a traditionalist in his theology. He did not approach the Nicene
Creed with the practiced skepticism of the historian of
dogma, who seeks to find there the traces of the various
theological schools and evidences of political compromise between them. But he was not only a traditionalist,
he was a traditionalist who sought to restate the traditional material in a manner that was relevant and contemporary. He by-passed elements in the Creed which
were most important to the controversialists who
wrote it, in favor of those elements in it that lent
themselves to existential reinterpretation. The greatness of the *Mass* lies in the fact that it managed to
take the full measure of the tradition without losing
itself in archaeology; neither iconoclasm nor idolatry
can be laid to its charge.[20] Bach believed that as the
medium of a historical faith, Christian art had to be
cast in terms of the historical repository of its tradition, but that as an expression of faith in the living
God, it had to be relevant and contemporary in its
use of this repository.

The fourth thesis is closely related to the third: *Christian art did not have a primarily programmatic function
in relation to the Word, but it could illuminate or even
transcend the content of the words with which it was
joined.* It was nēver Bach's intention to set his art in
competition with the Word, for the communication of
the Word of God was principally through the proclamation. In this sense, though he seems to go too far, Brunner is correct when he says: "The message of what God

---

[20]On the *Mass*, see the statement of W. Heim, quoted in Besch, *op.
cit.*, p. 167.

has done for our redemption certainly cannot be expressed as music, and what God wills to say to us in Jesus Christ cannot be painted. In this respect the human word is not simply one method among others, for human speech alone can indicate quite unambiguously God's thought, will, and work." Bach's Lutheran faith would have agreed with this judgment, for he regarded music as a response to what God had spoken in the Word. During the hour-long sermon at Leipzig, members of the choir were permitted to leave the cold church and warm themselves in the school, but in the school they had to read a sermon, that the Word might reach them anyway.[21] Bach appears to have been satisfied with this arrangement, for it meant that the members of the chorus, who were to render praise to God, would also hear the Word of God addressed to them. What a contrast this is to those who would confuse the sensory impact of color, line, or rhythm with the presence of the Holy Spirit, or who would receive the assurance of the forgiveness of sins from an A-flat on the clarinet!

Yet when all this has been said, as it must be, the fact remains that the kerygma is reinforced by its association with other media of communication. The prime example of this, in a class by themselves, are the sacraments, in which external means are the bearers of that grace which is the content of the kerygma. They are not to be understood apart from the kerygma, yet they bear its grace with a special connotation all their own. There is an analogous and quasi-sacramental function

---

[21]Emil Brunner, *The Divine Imperative*, trans. by Olive Wyon (Philadelphia, 1947), p. 502.

to Christian art, too. Dependent for its validation upon
the Word, it can nevertheless bring the Word in its
own special way and thus aid in its communication. In
the technique of doing this, Johann Sebastian Bach was
a master.[22]

One function that Bach's music performed in relation
to the text was the illumination of contrasts either implicit or explicit in the text. One such contrast in the
text of the *Mass* was that between the second "Kyrie"
and the "Gloria in excelsis." After the worshiper had
thrice begged for the forgiving mercy of his Lord in
plaintive assurance, he was moved to break forth:
"Gloria in excelsis Deo!" The contrast of mood between
the closing strains of the "Kyrie" and the opening bars
of the "Gloria" makes the suggestion appropriate that
"it is better to interpose a fairly long pause between
them, during which orchestra, choir, and audience can
traverse in silence the ground between the *Kyrie* and
the *Gloria*, and ascend from the depths of the minor
to the heights of the major harmonies from which, with
the first D major chords, the world of praise and thanksgiving will be opened out before them."[23] It must unfortunately be added that the entire meaning of this
contrast is usually lost when this interval is devoted to
the entree of the latecomers who feel able to listen de-
voutly to a "Gloria" without having first participated
in a "Kyrie." But the contrast is there nonetheless.

Another such contrast in the *Mass* came during the

[22]For a general treatment, cf. Arnold Schering, *Bachs Textbehand-
lung* (Leipzig, 1900), which is useful even for the reader without
technical competence.
[23]Schweitzer, *op. cit.*, II, 315.

second article of the "Credo." The setting of the "Cruci-
fixus etiam pro nobis sub Pontio Pilato, passus et sepultus est," articulated a grief seemingly beyond consolation. Unlike some preachers and theologians who relieve all too quickly their narration of the events of the
via dolorosa, Bach made the contrast between "passus
et sepultus est" and "Et resurrexit" so profound and so
brilliant that the hearer can hardly catch his breath
and is filled with awe. Here, in painful beauty, the majesty of the Holy in contrast to all that men could do
was trumpeted forth: "Et resurrexit tertia die . . . Cujus
regni non erit finis." A similar treatment appears in the
third article of the Creed, where Bach caught a significant contrast that a few commentators have noted in the
Nicene Creed. "Confiteor unum baptisma in remis-
sionem peccatorum" became an occasion for him to con-
template the reality of sin and the inevitability of death,
rather than merely an opportunity to rejoice in baptism.
And then slowly, as if not too quickly to disturb the
penance, the strings and voices moved up to "Expecto
resurrectionem mortuorum," which finally tears itself
loose from all preoccupation with death and sin in an
ecstatic outburst.

This same chorus illustrates another way that Bach
illumined the meaning of the text, by bringing out implicit relationships between various parts of the text
that might otherwise be missed. The "Expecto resurrectionem" in the third article was an echo of the "Et
resurrexit" in the second. The theological basis of this is
sound: in the New Testament, the Christ whom God
raised was the *aparche*, the first fruits, and those who

followed derived the power of their resurrection from His. God raised Him and raised us together with Him, so that we are assured of the "vita venturi saeculi" by the fact that God raised Him from the dead. In an eighteenth century that was emphasizing the theory of the natural immortality of the soul as basic to both common sense and Christian faith, Bach asserted the utterly contrary doctrine of the resurrection of the body, in which God had to intervene and had intervened by raising Christ. By his setting of the "Et expecto resurrectionem mortuorum" Bach reminded his hearers that the source of this expectation was the resurrection of the Second Adam, the new Head of the human race. There was a similar echo in the relation between "Gratias agimus" and the closing chorus of the *Mass*, "Dona nobis pacem." The peace for which this chorus prayed was that peace which the world could not give, for it was a peace that came only in a life that gave thanks to God—but gave thanks to Him for His great glory! And it acknowledged that this peace was a gift from the God who was glorious and lifted up, the God in Christ to whom the bass solo had sung: "Quoniam Tu solus sanctus, Tu solus Dominus."

In addition to bringing out contrasts and implicit relationships in the texts he set to music, Bach also illumined the text by bringing out its full scope and meaning. In the *Mass*, this function of the music comes into evidence in the "Benedictus" and the "Agnus Dei," which Bach managed to relate very effectively to his whole conception of the mass. Schweitzer has noted the differ-

ence between Bach and Beethoven at this point.[24] A
similar uniqueness is evident in Bach's treatment of the
words of institution in the *St. Matthew Passion*. Remem-
bered by the church from the earliest days and subjected to many music settings, the scene of the first cele-
bration of the Eucharist acquired here a solemnity that
removed it from the events immediately surrounding it
and reminded the church of His promise that He would
eat this Supper with them again in the kingdom of His
Father. Here again Bach's genius defied convention and
gave his music an abiding significance and his text a
permanent meaning.

This Bach did when he dealt with the sacred text of
the Gospels or Psalms, or when he set to music the
traditional text of the mass. He faced a different problem when he took up the texts supplied by contemporaries like Picander and Franck. Some few of these
texts are poetic gems and gave him an opportunity to
combine text, tune, and theology in a memorable fash-
ion. An outstanding example occurs in the *St. John
Passion*, whose dramatic movement is climaxed not in
the offering of a sacrificial victim to the wounded honor
of God, as Western theology traditionally interpreted
the Cross and the atonement, but in the victory of the
Cross: "Der Held aus Juda siegt mit Macht und schliesst
den Kampf. Es ist vollbracht." But most texts from
Bach's own period reflect a sentimentality most
accurately designated as maudlin. It was in the
use of these texts that the master really emerged.

---

[24]*Ibid.*, p. 323; on Bach's doctrine of resurrection, cf. Besch, *op. cit.*,
pp. 268 ff.

"Bluete nur, du liebes Herze" and "Zerfliesse, mein Herze in Fluten der Zaehren" are good examples from the texts of the two *Passions*. In both, a faithful following of the texts would have produced the kind of melody usually associated with such sentiments in the Pietist hymnody of the time. Instead, Bach set them to melodies that transcended them and gave them a solidity and strength transmuting them into positive confessions of Christian faith. In the same way, Cantata 161 used the chorale melody "Herzlich tut's mich verlangen" to change a baroque assertion of the liberation of the soul from the body into a more profoundly Christian confession than the text would permit.[25] Although Christian art did not have a primarily programmatic function in relation to the Word, it could illuminate or even transcend the content of the words with which it was joined.

In these and other ways, Bach was led by the overpowering mercy and overwhelming grace of the Holy to acknowledge a new dimension of life and value. The Holy is not, first of all, a highest Good, a sublimely True, an ultimately Beautiful. Yet that Holy which men have vainly tried to grasp with their systems of thought, their categories of ethics, and their depictions of beauty; that Holy which has eluded every human attempt to take it captive and to tame it; that Holy which is not the answer to every riddle but itself the enigma in every riddle—that Holy has been made flesh and has dwelt among us in Jesus Christ. He is the way,

---

[25]Cf. Martin Dibelius, "Individualismus und Gemeindebewusstsein in Joh. Seb. Bachs Passionen," *Botschaft und Geschichte, Gesammelte Aufsaetze*, ed. by Guenther Bornkamm, I (Tuebingen, 1953), 359-380.

the truth, and the life. He is the channel of the goodness of God. He is more beautiful than the children of men. Through Him God has redeemed all things to himself, including the True, the Good, and the Beautiful. On this rock of offense and stone of stumbling, human conceptions of truth and goodness and beauty have all been shattered. Yet this stone, which the builders of human systems rejected, has become instead the cornerstone for the dwelling-place of the Most High and Most Holy, from whom there proceeds all that is True and Good and Beautiful. Those who have despaired of the effort to domesticate the Holy, those whom He has led to know True and Good and Beautiful in Him—those are the "fools for Christ."

CPSIA information can be obtained
at www.ICGtesting.com
Printed in the USA
BVHW05s0720310718
523055BV00010B/96/P